THROUGH COUGAR'S

EYES

David !

Friendships last

FOREVER !!

Your friends,

THROUGH COUGAR'S
EYES

Life Lessons from One Man's Best Friend

DAVID RABER

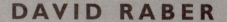

THOMAS DUNNE BOOKS

St. Martin's Press ❧ New York

THOMAS DUNNE BOOKS.
An imprint of St. Martin's Press.

www.stmartins.com

Grateful acknowledgment is given for permission to reprint letters as
follows: from Jerry L. Hill on page 141; from Peter F. Veling on
pages 179–180; from R. Avery Bennett on page 195.

All wildlife photos of Cougar by Greg Glass and Robert Philhower,
AGI Photographic Imaging, and courtesy of the Iams Company. All
other photos courtesy of David Raber and Linda Livingston.

Library of Congress Cataloging-in-Publication Data

Raber, David.
    Through Cougar's eyes : life lessons from one man's best friend /
    David Raber.—1st ed.
        p. cm.
    ISBN 0-312-26918-8
        1. Puma—Florida—Biography. 2. Pumas as pets—
Florida. 3. Raber, David. I. Title.

QL737.C23 R25 2001
636.8'9—dc21

                                                    00-050854

First Edition: April 2001

10 9 8 7 6 5 4 3 2 1

CONTENTS

ACKNOWLEDGMENTS

To Linda, thank you for putting up with and believing in me for sixteen years and counting.

To my book agent, Luna Carne-Ross, who over the years has become my best friend without our ever meeting.

To Peter Wolverton, Carolyn Dunkley, and a host of others at Thomas Dunne Books, and to Janet Fletcher, copy editor, and to Joseph Rinaldi, publicity manager, who together not only made the editing process a pure delight but also helped strengthen the book.

To all those souls who over the years understood and believed in Cougar.

And finally to Cougar, thank you for tolerating my human ways.

THROUGH COUGAR'S
EYES

INTRODUCTION

MANY PET "OWNERS" consider themselves experts on animals or at the very least are outspoken in their opinions about them. I am not an animal trainer. I am not an expert. But I am perceptive. I grew up with lots of animals, among them Westies, my sister's silver Persians, and even a housebroken rabbit named Thumper. Every spring I purchased a chameleon from the circus; then eventually I "owned" hamsters and parakeets—Mom put her foot down at my request for snakes. Though I regarded these animals as family, they were family in name only. They were pets and, as such, had their place.

This is normal . . . isn't it? I mean, isn't it normal to "own" an animal with little concern about passing it from owner to owner? Or is it human bias to presume animals are a lower life form without intense emotions, and that we are making them happy? Could it be that happiness is more complicated than a full belly and a scratch behind the ear? Is it human arrogance to assume that only we are complex? Could what we see as pets' simple natures be merely a reflection of our elementary understanding of them?

In a benevolent dictatorship the ruler seldom understands or relates to his subjects. Actually, most rulers don't wish to understand, but just keep their subjects in line, sometimes with fear. A relationship is different, though. It is an equality depending on understanding and connecting, not fear. For sovereigns, closer ties require that they take the first step, recognize that though smarter in some ways, they are less smart in others. Unfortunately, this rarely happens because rulers tend to be egotists who believe that dominating is their right. But by understanding, a ruler no longer has to demand—just ask. So by dominating, the ruler has security, but through understanding he has lasting peace. Is ruling an animal any different?

I grew up continuing to believe that pets were special, but animals just the same. Then something extraordinary happened. I rescued a mountain lion—Cougar—and he saved me. I learned to look at the world through his eyes and found out that he was extremely intelligent, though in ways different from us, and that he was just as emotional as I was. This relationship would refocus my priorities and change what I had considered important. Eventually I would recognize the importance to all of us of becoming good neighbors with wildlife, of learning to coexist gracefully with animals. I then wanted to educate people to the fact that mountain lions and other animals are to be respected, not feared, that they are an essential part of the environment. I hoped that maybe the magnificence of nature, and particularly the innocence of its many inhabitants, would touch an inner core in my fellow humans—not only benefiting animals but people, too.

To achieve my goal, I needed to bring Cougar to people. In order for me to do this he needed to act naturally, to be comfortable with us as well as with wildlife—a big job and a bigger responsibility. But then I wondered, What about house cats? They, too, are intelligent and naturally curious: So what happens when they live indoors? Do they become afraid of the outdoors, or do they still have the natural feline traits? It's true that cats living in apartments in large cities cannot go outdoors without the risk of getting lost or being run over, but they still need stimulation and fun to be totally happy and well adjusted; otherwise they become victims of mental stagnation.

Happiness is complicated. The only way to help create it in another individual is to relate to him: talk his talk and walk his walk. This requires looking at the world through his eyes. And if it's a feline you're dealing with, that takes even more effort. Take store-bought cat toys, for example: Do they bring pleasure to your cat, or to you? How many times does your cat find something else to play with? Thinking human may bring pleasure to you, but not necessarily to your cat.

But I want to make humans happy, too, and educate them. I want to enlighten the encroachers concerning the plight of wildlife, help them realize that "wild" is a label we use to describe something we don't understand, as we did with Native Americans at the turn of the previous century. The Native Americans believed that they were an integral part of nature—tenants, not conquerors. Now, one hundred years later, we are just catching on. I maintain that no one can conquer anything he or she doesn't understand. Many times, however, it seems we have just enough knowledge to get ourselves into trouble. Call it conceit. As powerful as we believe ourselves to be with our spacecraft, communications satellites, and so forth, it's really just a matter of perspective. A hundred years ago we felt the same confidence about other issues, and a hundred years from now we will still feel that we are the ones in control. But Mother Nature has always had the upper hand—a universal power. In our technical world, taking a backseat, even to Mother Nature, is demeaning. But a backseat based on knowledge is better than a front seat based on ignorance. It's humility versus insolence. We cage Mother Nature, mow her down, contaminate her, and she forgives us. But ironically, the more we hurt her, the more we suffer.

WHEN I STARTED living with Cougar and developing these thoughts, I wondered where he had come from, how his ancestors had fared, and I started reading up on that. One of the books that I found very helpful and informative was *Cougar: The American Lion*, by Kevin Hansen in association with the Mountain Lion Foundation, with a Foreword by Robert Redford (Flagstaff, Arizona: Northland Publishing, 1992).

The names "mountain lion" (from European settlers), "cougar" (from Brazilian Indians), "panther" (Greek for leopard), "painter" (American colloquial for panther), "puma" (from Inca Indians), "mountain screamer" (pioneer expression), "catamount" (New England term meaning cat-of-the-mountains), "deer cat" (referring to the most common prey), "American cat" (because it is the only widespread large cat of the Americas), and ninety-some other names used in different geographic locations refer to the same species of cat: *Felis concolor*, cat of one color. This cat has more names listed in dictionaries than any other animal in the world, and it's no wonder. He is elusive and inclusive, calling North, Central, and South America home. He has the largest territorial range of any animal in the Western hemisphere and is comfortable from sea level to 14,765 feet, whether in dense forests of the Pacific Northwest, in arid deserts of the Southwest, or in the Florida Everglades. He is resilient and adaptable—barring the arrival of "white eyes."

It all started in the fourteenth century, when Europeans first trampled his shores. Early colonists considered him a threat to civilization, livestock, and game; thus he was not only shot on sight but aggressively hunted and trapped. More threatening, though, was the loss of his habitat. Increasingly confined by agriculture, towns, cities, and roads, he has been pushed back—in North America alone—to twelve western states, the Canadian provinces of British Columbia and Alberta, and in Southern Florida, where there is a small remnant population estimated to be no more than fifty.

Modern man wasn't a problem fifty million years ago for miacids—the primitive, tree-dwelling carnivores of the Northern Hemisphere that were ancestors to the mountain lion. Ten million years later, two modern families of carnivores evolved: arctoids, bearlike predecessors of the bear, otter, dog, raccoon, lesser panda, badger, and weasel, and a catlike group, aeluroids, predecessors of cats, hyenas, genets, civets, and the mongoose.

Thirty-five million years ago, the saber-toothed cat appeared and reigned until the end of the last glaciation, only ten thousand years ago. Two million years ago ancestral cougars evolved, and the modern mountain lion originated one million, nine hundred thousand years later, just one hundred thousand years in the past.

Felines are now broadly categorized into two genera: *Panthera*, the large roaring cats, and *Felis*, the smaller purring cats. Roaring and purring are generated by a hyoid bone in the cats' larynx, or voice box. The mountain lion is the largest purring cat.

The cougar is widely distributed, and it exhibits regional variations brought on by differing habitats. Differences in size, color, cranial details, and dental structure have produced twenty-six subspecies, twelve of which reside in North America.

IT ALL GETS started when a male and female mountain lion spend a week or two together, mating perhaps sixty times a day. About ninety-three days later, the pregnant female, contrary to the scenario of many nature movies, prepares the simplest of dens, providing only temporary and rudimentary protection against transient cougars, coyotes, golden eagles, heavy rain, and hot sun.

One to six one-pound, spotted, blue-eyed kittens, also called cubs, squeak into the world, latching onto and generally claiming one of their mother's six milk-producing nipples out of a total of eight. Just after a week has passed, their eyes open. At two weeks old, they have doubled their weight and are awkwardly exploring rocks, brush, or an overhang they might call home. This is when the mother has to hunt—a time when her kittens are vulnerable. Consequently, a home range for her should have plentiful prey and cover and, ideally, be twenty-five square miles in size. A larger territory of several hundred square miles in size would be much less suitable, forcing her to be away for prolonged periods of time.

A mother cougar begins by carrying meat to her cubs; then, when they are still as young as seven to eight weeks of age, she starts leading them to kills. As the kittens become stronger and more adroit, she will take them farther and farther in search of prey, and she will continue doing so until they are fully weaned, at between two and three months of age, when they weigh between seven and nine pounds. By now they have moved several times—maybe setting an example that their home is the entire territory, and the stars are their roof.

Teeth and coat are critical to survival. Baby canines appear when the kittens are three weeks old, and molars follow two weeks later. Permanent teeth begin pushing their way through at around five months.

A spotted coat best camouflages an animal at rest, and thus is perfectly suited for the vulnerable kittens. Around twelve to fourteen weeks of age these spots begin to fade. During this time, the adolescent cat is on the move, learning to hunt—a situation favoring a monotone coat. At early adulthood, around fifteen months, the spots are only light smudges on the hindquarters, seen only if the light hits them just right.

And eye color is changing too. From a bright azure blue at birth the cubs' eyes begin transforming at four months of age to gold. This process will be completed at the same time the spots fully disappear—around sixteen months.

The site of a kill becomes a virtual playground for the cubs: flattened grass, broken limbs, clawed tree trunks, and bits of hair and bone are everywhere. There is nothing left but the memories when they follow their mother in search of other prey.

Then one day the young adult cubs, twelve to eighteen months old, might be gnawing on a carcass, swatting their brothers and sisters as before, but this time their mother does not return. Hunger motivates them to disperse. They are now transients. When they settle in a new territory, they are called residents, until displaced or killed—usually by man.

UNFORTUNATELY, MOST MOUNTAIN lions are killed by us, whether intentionally or unintentionally. Not only do we encroach on their territory, we shoot, poison, trapp, and snare them. Today cougar hunting is legal in Arizona, Colorado, Idaho, Montana, Nevada, New Mexico, Oregon, Texas, Utah, Washington, Wyoming, and the Canadian provinces of British Columbia and Alberta. Most states limit hunters to one lion, though the limit is difficult to enforce. Texas has no legal limits. How shortsighted can Texans be, allowing indiscriminate hunting, while not far away, in Florida, the panther is the state animal and protected? The Florida panther is endangered and the Texas cougar is shot on sight. Can we be so different?

Hunters have long rationalized that they are doing nature a favor, for without them, they say, the mountain lion would reduce deer populations and compromise their "sport." But in the 1960s Dr. Maurice Hornocker radio-collared mountain lions and proved undisputably that the lions self-regulate their numbers. When prey is abundant, the lions produce more offspring, and when prey numbers are meager, mountain lion families shrink accordingly. It's all in the natural scheme of things. I don't believe nature needs our help. We kill animals, calling it sport, but if they attack us, it's wild behavior. Let's declare hunting what it really is: a premeditated act to harm.

Ironically, the greatest rationalization used by hunters in-

vokes camaraderie and family tradition. The enjoyment of getting away—the fresh air and fellowship—is a tradition passed
down from generation to generation. Aside from acknowledging
the fact that extraterrestrials could make the same argument for
hunting us, we should ask: Does man have an instinctive desire to
kill, or does he do it just because he can? There is no logical reason except that, to some, hunting is "exciting." But why not experience the same positive emotion by shooting film instead? We
know that animals feel pain and experience emotion. Why should
causing them physical and emotional pain be enjoyable? We have
all experienced emotional pain and dealt with it the best way
possible. Only our closest friends knew. Are animals any different? When they are emotionally stressed, why not believe that
they too deal with tragedy subtly? Why consider them beneath
us? With that mind-set, believing that certain people are inferior
is just around the corner. And if we want "sport," why not com-
pete on a playing field with those who can understand and accept
the rules, where the odds are even, and where no one gets killed?

Even without the menace of man, cougars' lives are extremely
difficult. Cougars prey on animals that are much larger than
themselves. An elk, for example, is seven times larger. Cougars
are thrown into trees, trampled by hooves, and impaled on
branches or antlers. Deer are the prey of choice, and, though
smaller than elk, they are still quick with hooves and antlers.
Almost any injury, such as a broken jaw, is life-threatening to a
cougar.

So the mountain lion doesn't have it easy—anywhere—
whether in the nonexistent "wild" or in a cage. Either way, he
is dominated by us. It's just a matter of degree. Will he be "born

free," to be run over, shot, or starved? Or will his life be more confined, born in a cage to die in a cage? We humans compromise both existences.

I WANT THE best of both worlds for Cougar. I want to love and learn about this magnificent fellow, dispelling myth, learning how to help him and us, too. It is Cougar and my relationship with him that has brought out the best in me. He has shown me the way. I am at peace and wish the same for other people, Cougar, and his cousins.

RESCUING IS NEVER PLANNED

COUGAR'S STORY BEGINS without me. . . .

It was frosty late September on a northern Wisconsin farm midway between Eau Claire and Wausau. Brisk weather isn't so bad when you're cozy and warm. But an eighteen-by-thirty-foot chain-link cage with only a small, makeshift wooden enclosure to help block upcoming winter winds was the home provided for a pair of cougars. Certainly not cozy, but most would say that's not important. In a smaller cage there was a solitary black bear who wailed as corn rippled in the distance and cows ruminated, breath streaming from warm, moist nostrils, which dissipated into the evening stillness. At least no one was starving.

These animals were caged for one reason, breeding. Their cubs would supplement the meager farm income of Dean, Joyce, and their fourteen-year-old son.

Of the two cougars, Nigel was a handsomely regal cat, tawny in color just like a deer, with golden eyes. His mustache, his ears, and the tip of his tail were coal black; his muzzle, chin, and chest were bright as snow. The contrasting mustache and muzzle are distinguishing characteristics of cougars, mountain lions, pumas, and panthers. Nigel was seven years old and weighed more than 300 pounds. He was mammoth by mountain lion standards, though 25 percent of his weight was the fat of inactivity. He'd weigh a trim 250 stalking and capturing prey, but here all he had to do was devour the road-killed deer or slaughtered cows heaved into his cage. Even if he was hungry, which was seldom, Nigel would wait for his mate, Sabrina, to finish eating; then he'd polish off what was left, which was enough to keep his paunch swinging just inches from the ground.

Sabrina, who was five years old, weighed a much trimmer 125 pounds, which was still large for a female. She had smooth, graceful lines and soft eyes. Cougar females look identical to the males except for being smaller, but this autumn evening Sabrina was bulging. Ninety-three days ago she and Nigel had mated, and now it was time to bear her young.

On Dean and Joyce's farm, both humans and cats just existed. Granted, Nigel and Sabrina were well fed. Their owners weren't hungry either, but extravagances like a recreational vehicle, a boat, or a motorcycle (except for a rusty, inoperable hand-me-down leaning silently against the barn wall) were all but non-existent, except in dreams. And dreams ran rampant, because Sabrina was about to deliver three to four furry bundles of tawny fur with dark brown spots, ringed tails, and azure eyes.

It was early evening on September 29, 1990, when Sabrina knew it was time. Nigel recognized that something was up, for Sabrina was uncharacteristically standoffish and didn't tolerate his being close, which in the cage was everywhere.

Though Nigel was more than twice Sabrina's size, he honored her wish for solitude. He tried to melt into the corner, lay down, watched, and waited. It wasn't long before Sabrina sought the privacy of the enclosure. Shortly thereafter, minute cheeping noises emerged from inside. Nigel was curious; after all, the scent was his. But when he approached, Sabrina lashed out with a vengeance.

Dean and Joyce heard the commotion and quickly bolted from the farmhouse. This was it: payday! Dean knew what to do. He grabbed a rope, tied it into a noose, hastened over to the cage door, unlatched it, and stepped through. After closing the chain-link door behind him, he walked slowly over to Nigel, who didn't mind being led around on a rope. Dean slipped the loop over Nigel's head, tightened the noose, and led him from the cage to an enclosure so small that Nigel had difficulty turning around.

Over the next several days, Nigel watched from his casketlike retreat as Sabrina and her kittens were on display. She was uncomfortable. In her fishbowl existence she nervously groomed her family, as neighbors came by to gawk. But she wasn't the only one tending to others.

Dean was calling potential clients, people interested in buying mountain lion cubs for three hundred and fifty bucks each. Dean wished Sabrina had more offspring, but three was better than none. At least after paying their most critical bills, he could get that fishing rod, or buy Joyce a bracelet, or their son that .22 rifle. Thankfully, Nigel and Sabrina caused little expense.

Deer hit on the road or slaughtered cows sufficed as food. And there were no veterinary bills. After all, there were no doctors in the wild. The boy did much of the feeding and cage cleaning after school. All Dean had to do, other than the unending farmwork, was sell the animals.

Dean had heard about a pet dealer from Indianapolis who

dealt in exotic animals. That summer, after discovering that Sabrina was pregnant, Dean had called him. The dealer was particularly excited about the timing of a "Christmas cub." And there was a private individual in North Carolina who was interested in another. That was two. Dean knew it was common, for newborn cubs to die, but he lined up a third potential buyer just in case all three survived. It was unwise to count chickens before they hatched or mountain lions before they were shipped. And sometimes even shipping didn't mean he got his money.

Twelve days later it was time for Joyce to be a surrogate mother, time these two little guys and one gal were beginning to open their eyes. So Dean heaved a recently killed deer into the corner of Sabrina's cage. He knew she would be hungry. She glanced at the carcass, stared as if waiting for it to move, then got up, stretched, yawned, and strolled over to it.

Joyce cautiously entered the cage. Without once taking her eyes off Sabrina, she eased her way to the opening of the enclosure. Three squirming kittens lay inside. She quickly snatched all three. They screeched in defiance. Sabrina paused, then continued eating. Joyce quickly let herself out of the cage, feeling much better on the other side of the door. She knew that if these cubs survived, something would forever haunt them—a persistent longing for something soft and warm to suckle, especially when menaced. Then they would mound up whatever was available, and pretend to nurse in order to feel comfortable again.

Joyce felt a twinge of guilt but knew these kittens were for humans. The more their mom taught them, the more catlike they would become. So Joyce fought her feelings, thinking instead about the money. For the next six weeks she would cradle and bottle-feed the cubs cow's milk—would *be* their mother until they were sold.

Dean had always marked cattle by cutting a triangle from each animal's ear. Thinking there was little difference between cattle and cats, Dean walked over to the kitchen drawer, grabbed a pair of large scissors, stepped up to the cubs' makeshift corrugated cardboard home, and proceeded to notch the left ear of each kitten. They squirmed, then screamed. Outside, Sabrina looked up and froze.

This process of tending to their investment continued for a month and a half until the pet merchant from Indianapolis called. Both Dean and Joyce knew it was too soon to transport the cubs. They needed to be weaned, and that would take at least two more weeks. It was even against federal regulations to ship cubs less than eight weeks old. But Dean and Joyce weren't licensed. They couldn't lose a license they didn't have. Besides, who would know? These cubs were their property and the pet merchant had money . . . and their unpaid bills were as stifling as the scent of manure, so Dean checked on the next flight to Indianapolis.

Joyce walked out to the shed, dusted off a dilapidated animal carrier, and brought it inside. She found a tattered bath towel and arranged it in the bottom. Early the next morning it was time for her to select the plumpest kitten, bottle-feed him until he nearly burst, fluff the towel in the carrier, and place him inside. It would be time for his next feeding when Dean dropped him at the airport. Then time for another feeding when the plane he was on landed in Chicago. Then time for another feed-

ing before the next takeoff. Then time for another feeding before arrival at his final destination, Indianapolis.

A listless, hungry, dehydrated cub was claimed by the pet
merchant and his assistant in midafternoon. They thought he
was cute, not knowing his eyes were dry and his squeaks deeper
than usual. If only they knew how important it was to feed him!
But instead they drove to the store and put him on display. He
was finally fed a bottle of milk in early evening, more for show
than anything else. And by closing time he had a low-grade
fever.

The next morning he had diarrhea. The combination of
missing his home, being cold, skipping four successive feedings,
the terrifying hissing noise caused by pressurization of the aircraft's cargo hold, the high-pitched whine of the jet engines, and
the bright lights when he was on display and constantly being
handled was debilitating. He just wanted it to be the way it was.
But it wouldn't be. A pet merchant, not even licensed to sell
exotic animals, would see to that.

This was this cub's miserable existence for three days. His
temperature inched higher and his strength declined. Eventually
he didn't want his bottle. The employee assigned to open the
store the next morning was not met with the usual chirps, just
silence. Peering inside the cub's cage, she realized that this little
guy had gathered a section of towel up into a mound and pre-
tended to suckle until he died.

She immediately called the pet merchant, who then called
Dean, complaining that the cub had died, demanding either a
replacement or his money. Dean assured him that he would send
another cub, which would arrive the following day. At least,

Dean thought, the remaining two were weaned. And they were so different. The male always took control while his sister just sat back. Dean felt that, of the two, the stronger personality was needed to survive the trip; consequently, he selected the determined male.

Without another carrier, Dean had to construct a crate out of spare lumber. The crate, however, wasn't the only thing different. With seven more days of care than his deceased sibling had had, this little fellow was more coordinated and heavier. More important, though, he was a survivor.

Joyce repeated the preparations for the trip. But this time a chicken leg accompanied the cub in his cage while he was driven to the airport. He missed his home as he waited for his crate to be loaded into an airplane. He was cold. He was terrified of the hissing noises. He was frightened being transferred from one aircraft to another in Chicago. He was scared when the aircraft dropped, feeling his stomach tumbled with it. He was terrified, just as his brother had been. But after arriving in Indianapolis, he felt more determined than weak. He wasn't taking all this sitting down . . . and who were these folks calling him cutie?

The pet merchant and his assistant peered into the cub's crate and cooed. They remembered a lethargic specimen of a mountain lion kitten—one who, because of their selfishness and stupidity, eventually died. But this little guy was a tornado on paws. He didn't want to be handled, even hissed when they tried. He had an attitude; they called him obstinate. But labels weren't important, selling him was. He would have to be "cuddly." The Christmas expo at the Indianapolis Convention Center was the day after tomorrow. He would have to be drugged.

The local newspaper, after finding out that a mountain lion cub was to be one of the extravagant gifts on display, sent a photographer to the pet shop. He found the store was packed with intrigued patrons and, after readying his camera, snapped pictures of an assistant posed with the feature attraction, who, with half-opened eyes, just rested his chin on her forearm. Everyone thought the cub to be cuddly; the photographer was the only one to observe how sleepy he was. The cub's picture appeared in the paper the following day, a cub seemingly resting in the arms of his benefactor and gazing blankly into the distance, eyelids drooping. This entire situation is deplorable, but mountain lions have no rights in a human world.

IN NATURE, MOUNTAIN lions generally don't have it much better, living three or four years before being hit by a car or chased up a tree by dogs to be shot by a hunter. In captivity, they may live to be twenty. But can twenty years in a cage be considered living? The destiny of this particular kitten was to have the best of both worlds, be safe from cars and bullets, yet free. Drugged and crammed into a toaster-size cage, he waited.

MY NAME IS David Raber. Riding a motorcycle, racing a car or boat, and flying an airplane are all natural for me; it's as if I was born to do these things. They require being one with the machine and an ability to feel what's going to happen before it does. This perception works on people, too. I watch them closely, intently observing, believing actions mean more than words. This could make people uneasy, but usually doesn't. It's a trait that has assisted me both personally and in business. Flying was my business and my love until I was diagnosed with diabetes and permanently grounded. Doctors with diabetes can still perform surgery but pilots are not allowed to fly. So my wings were clipped, and if I can't do what I'm best at, if I can't be the best at what I'm doing, then it's not fun anymore.

Linda is my girlfriend and significant other—a five-foot-two brunette who makes a 105-pound Sicilian model look like a mere spin-off. We met ten years before this story begins, but nothing clicked between us. Two years later, however, when we bumped into each other in a crowded nightclub, she reminded me that we'd met before and fired off a dozen reasons why I should remember, too. Taken aback, but intrigued, I invited her to fly to Hilton Head for the weekend, and we've been together ever since.

Linda settled in with me and enjoyed the extravagant lifestyle I was then able to provide, though possessions certainly weren't important to her. Unfortunately, she got a chance to prove that when, because of diabetes, I was unable to fly for a living and my over-leveraged lifestyle quickly brought me to my knees. Economically, we tumbled together. I knew I'd recover, physically and financially, and Linda had faith, but neither of us realized how long this recovery would take.

Having money has never been important to me. Money just happens because I do what I love to do. I adored flying and enjoyed the resulting income, but that was out and my life was changing. To boost our spirits, Linda and I decided to visit the Indianapolis Convention Center where, during the Christmas holidays, they had a show displaying extravagant gifts—luxury yachts and cars and so on. It would be fun and therapeutic. We couldn't afford to buy anything, but so what? It's the thought of things to be and then making them happen that counts. So as a couple accustomed to flying high in private aircraft and low in fast cars, we bought two tickets and walked through the doors. A bright red Ferrari was sitting just inside the entrance. It was almost hypnotic—this red rocket on wheels. We circled it, both of us somehow believing it would just be a blink of an eye before we were again sporting about in a high-performance automobile, Pavarotti recordings buffeted by the wind, accompanied by the music that multiple herds of mechanical horses make.

We circled the car slowly, methodically, when there was a scream, not human in origin, but of a much higher pitch, something like a screech. What on earth was that? I thought, gazing in the general direction of the disturbance. It seemed I was being torn away from this tantalizing exoticness before me, drawn by an invisible force. It was like being beamed across the floor into another dimension. And before I knew it I was front and center in a group of approximately fifty people, with Linda at my side.

I've never considered myself an animal-rights type of person. Granted, being kind to animals was always important, but eating a hamburger or cutting down trees didn't bother me. What was in front of me right now, however, was disturbing: a wildlife kitten squeezed into a cage so small he was forced to stand as if in a miniature squeeze box. People were poking and prodding him. How could they do that? Couldn't they see this little guy was terrified? Apparently not, for what was important to them was touching for their pleasure. It reminded me of molestation. I can't watch rape scenes on television; it's easier to see a murder enacted. The powerlessness—the torture mixed with humilia-tion—makes it unbearable to watch, like what was happening in front of me right now. Abuse is abuse.

This was obviously a wildlife kitten, but what exactly? "Would you please take him out," I requested, half asking, half demanding. The plump assistant with long brownish-blond hair glanced over her shoulder toward her boss. He eyed me, glanced at my Rolex, and nodded. She grasped the cub, slid him back-wards out of his makeshift tomb, and handed him to me. So there I was, a man who didn't like cats, holding one. I mean, I was an admitted dog person. When I hollered, I wanted action, not a vertical tail telling me to get lost.

I was once given a tabby kitten—more my daughter's gift to herself—whom I named Regal. Regal was friendly and was little bother. But Chivas, a golden retriever, was my pride and joy. I impulsively got him eight years ago to help lick the sting of divorce away when my children were visiting.

Now all I could see were sky blue eyes rising over a pink nose. When I adjusted my arms, he wanted to bolt, so I held him carefully and, with Linda by my side, walked from the crowd, nonchalantly throwing a question over my shoulder: "What is he?"

"A mountain lion," the assistant answered. A mountain lion? I pondered. As a boy I drove my parents nuts, always asking why this or why that. Now I had a hundred questions and no one to ask.

When we'd walked to a quiet place, the cub scooted back into the crook of my arm. He seemed curious, not frightened. It wasn't long before I discovered a lonely pleasure boat on display off the beaten path, so I placed the kitten inside, allowing him to snoop around. Soon he was discovered. I motioned the intruders back and slowly picked him up, this time not by restraining but by scooping with an open hand. Who was training whom?

I knew I should take him back, but hesitated. Out of the corner of my eye I noticed a six-foot bench against the convention center wall. It would be just a little delay, I thought, more vacation time from his cage. I walked over and sat down. After I'd placed him next to me, he paused for a moment, then staggered away on the slanted, shellacked surface. It was funny how he kept sliding to the back of the bench. Soon a family of five appeared. This time the cub didn't wait, but skidded back and jumped into my lap. I felt an electrifying chill, an exhilarating, inspiring thrill. Everyone likes to be wanted, but this was more. I acknowledged his name in a whisper: "Hello, Cougar."

Oops! Linda had seen this before. I was either in neutral, or hair on fire streaking past Mach 2. Linda knew that whatever happened, I wouldn't accept anything short of perfection, but she had no idea where this was going. And, honestly, neither did I. The only thing important now was freeing him.

I got up slowly, so as not to disturb my passenger, and stepped toward a transformation, a lifestyle change, a process whereby I would learn to look at the world through Cougar's eyes and, in so doing, be able to relate. Linda gently scratched him behind the ear and he began to purr. It was easy to see he was happy. Keeping him that way for the rest of his life would be the challenge.

Back at the pet store display, I whispered for Linda to reach into my coat pocket for my wallet. She opened it and I nodded toward a card that I'd used in the past to buy anything I wanted, a card whose unpaid statements were piled high on my desk. She flung it on the counter. Would it be accepted?

The assistant swiped the now worthless piece of plastic through the machine. She hadn't seen a card like this one and seemed impressed as she examined it, then she smiled. I asked what to feed the kitten. Two pieces of raw chicken a day, she said. "That's it?" I asked. "That's it." But this merchant would have fed him dog food if it was cheaper. I'd rather find out for myself.

The din of the crowd became distant. If the card was declined, Cougar might end up cramped in a cage, God knows where, passed from one owner to the next—one abusive and another indifferent, one careless and another mean—until a cat born in a cage died in a cage. It was beyond being a waste. It was an outrage. I was holding my breath when a beep rang out from the credit card terminal. I had heard it a million times before, but this time was different. This was a life. Cougar was mine—or, as I would soon learn, I was his.

The assistant wrote the approval code on the two-thousand-dollar sales ticket and handed me the pen, saying she'd throw in the cage. So who needs a cage? I would have paid more—a ransom, or the cost of adoption. And I'll always wonder if I would have reacted the same with an "ordinary" house cat. The answer is probably no; after all, I wasn't even a cat person. It took a special cat to get my attention.

Now it was time to relish the success and not think about tomorrow. But there was a snag, the first of many. This kitten was expected to provide a significant draw for the show. The only way I would be allowed to take him home was if I agreed to return the next day; otherwise, I could pick him up Sunday night. Sure . . . like I was going to shove him back into that coffin! I agreed, but I'd do it my way: no more cages, no more petting, no more pet store. The pet store exhibitor accepted my terms.

IT WAS DARK outside, a below-zero evening. Snow fell with a silent, swirling rush that stuck to your eyelashes and squeaked under your shoes. The pet store assistant suggested that I put the kitten in his cage and throw the cage into the back of my truck. What a heart! Instead I handed Cougar to Linda and stood close until he was comfortable. Then I was directed to an emergency exit that not only was close by, but was only fifty yards from my duelie truck parked outside. I had used this truck the year before to pull my racing team's forty-foot trailer. This year, I was racing against time. After a quick jog to start the engine, I returned and Cougar chirped. It was my first lesson in mountain lion talk. Tonight it meant, "Hey, I missed you." Hundreds more translations, utilizing differences in intensity, volume, and pitch, were to follow.

When I zipped up my jacket around him, he didn't resist. I'm gaining on it, I thought. Cougar focused on the approaching emergency exit and wasn't startled when I pushed the bar and opened the door. Winter's wrath blasted against his little nose. But I didn't feel it—just the chill of excitement.

The drive home was exhilarating. I talked to Cougar in a high-pitched whisper while he watched streetlights, listened to the sound of traffic, and zeroed in on the occasional shadow leaning against the wind. Cougar seemed comfortable, as if he didn't have a concern in the world. And at the moment I had only one: Did he have to pee?

Twenty minutes later and still high and dry, I steered into the garage, hearing Chivas excitedly prancing on the kitchen floor just inside the door. I handed Cougar to Linda and asked her to remain in the car until I could "love on" Chivas to settle him down. And I'm glad I did, for after letting myself inside, I was immediately covered with canine welcome-homes. Even Regal joined in with his feline version. Their excitement was noticeably elevated by a new scent—small wonder. So after everything had settled down, I announced that I would like to make introductions. Chivas knew something was up. Regal played oblivious, but didn't move.

I walked back into the garage, picked up Cougar, and suggested that Linda precede me, so as to drain any remaining excitement from Chivas. And after opening the door only far enough to squeeze by, she bent down and loved both of her "boys." Then, when I could no longer hear the claw scratches on the kitchen floor, I opened the door and stood motionless. I had their undivided attention.

I bent down. Cougar's scent was electrifying to them. Chivas rammed his nose under Cougar and kept it there—as if he couldn't get enough—until Cougar had enough and swatted. Chivas backed up, hesitated, then thrust his nose back under Cougar, who looked like a broncobuster riding a bull. This went on for several seconds until Cougar finally landed a good hard swat, this time with a hiss. It got Chivas's attention, so he backed up and just stared—tail still wagging, tongue still dangling, and eyes darting back and forth, from me to Cougar.

Finally Chivas sat down and glanced at Linda, who was removing clean dishes from the dishwasher. It seemed that calmness prevailed, so I slowly placed Cougar on the floor. Cougar weighed approximately 7 pounds, Regal 11, and Chivas 115. To the kitten, Chivas must have looked like a horse, and Regal, just because he was an adult, could have been intimidating. This might have been the case, but Cougar saw it differently.

He confidently examined his surroundings and took a step. Chivas rushed forward. Cougar reared back on his haunches and struck him with all his might—a hard, lightening-fast blow with a spit for emphasis. Chivas was startled and Regal was petrified. Chivas backed up and shook his head. Regal didn't move, just glared. He was awestruck. With extreme trepidation Regal examined Cougar, staring first at his head, then down to his chest, his legs—then, as if hit by a bolt of lightening, he stood frozen with alarm, his eyes glued. Those paws! He'd never seen paws like pillows. They were huge! Regal bolted for cover.

From Cougar's standpoint that was two down and none to go. Time to explore. Chivas observed from a distance; Regal hid in a distant closet as Cougar quickly left the wooden kitchen floor for the beckoning call of carpet.

Cougar, as if on rails, walked directly over to the Scandinavian teak stereo cabinet that was Regal's favorite resting spot. It had just enough room underneath for a crouching feline to scooch, turn around, and plop down. Cougar tried it out. It was perfect. But curiosity took precedence; it was on to his next discovery: a large, highly polished, cylindrical copper stand with pictures displayed on top. Cougar lingered in front of his shiny reflection, making sure the image was him. After all, there was only room for one wildlife cat in these parts.

Cougar would soon discover the entire house, an expansive home with few walls and an informal atmosphere where there were vaulted ceilings; picture windows; a massive stone fireplace; many ficus trees and other plants; Remington bronzes; oil paintings; Doolittle nature prints; stained glass art; teak, oak, and cherry tables and chairs; blue and black leather armchairs and couches; Indian tapestries and carpets; stereo systems; silver trays; crystal decanters and glasses; and an outside pool with surrounding cedar deck. I loved this place and saw no earthly reason a mountain lion wouldn't fit in.

After all, it was now Cougar's home too. But there were problems. First, I had promised Cougar no more cages. Throwing him into a larger cage just didn't seem right. This pledge, however, didn't consider my current fondness for physical things. I adored my possessions. But Cougar took priority and eventually he would weigh two-hundred-plus pounds and be capable of jumping straight up twenty-eight feet and leaping forty-two feet. A cat, I would soon learn, was a chewer. And how about housebreaking?

But first things first: he looked hungry. Those creeps probably didn't feed him. Call me strange, but throwing food into a bowl seemed impersonal, especially when I was doing my best to get up close and personal. I admit to feeding Chivas and Regal out of bowls. So what was happening? For some reason a bowl didn't seem appropriate with Cougar; too detached. So I opened the refrigerator door, picked out the biggest and best piece of uncooked chicken, turned around, and almost tripped over Cougar. Smart boy, I thought. After plopping down and sitting cross-legged on the kitchen floor, I extended my arm, offering a chicken leg. "Do you like white or dark meat?" I whispered with a smile.

First he sniffed; then, with baby teeth bigger than Regal's adult set, he chomped into the meaty end with a crunch. I guess it doesn't matter, I thought. But I pondered again. I'll bet he does have a preference. And this chicken was raw. What about salmonella poisoning and the possibility of parasites? Most, I'm sure, would say that predators like Cougar are immune to such hazards, but how could I be sure? Who knows how mountain lions die in the wild? And how about chlorinated water?

After finishing off everything but my unanswered questions, Cougar scampered away. How would I corral all this energy? Maybe, at times, I could confine him to the solarium, which had a tile floor, wall-to-wall windows overlooking a forest, a bird feeder, and suet for squirrels. Lots of activity for mental stimulation, I thought. I would have to sleep on the idea. Hmm, and where would Cougar sleep? With me, of course. So after watching Cougar explore until after midnight, I lifted him up and carried him to my . . . and Linda's . . . and now Cougar's bedroom.

After much caressing, I laid him on the floor next to me and turned out the light. It wasn't long before he was sniffing my hand. Then he pounced on a stray foot moving under the covers. I picked him up, snuggled his face, and put him back on the floor. Seconds later he was back. Maybe there is room for him in bed, I thought. After all, this is a king-size water bed. Hmm.

I had visions of three inches of water cascading down the hall. Nah, never happen. So I pressed a comfortable impression into a king-size pillow, placed Cougar in the middle, lightly stroked him, put my head down, and went to sleep . . . for three hours.

I awoke to Cougar licking my arm. Had he been drugged, and was he now burning up all that pent-up energy? It was like he was on uppers. I stroked him until I fell asleep and started to snore. Then he sat on my face. Gosh, this cat was wound up tighter than a spool of thread; by comparison, Regal didn't move the entire night.

THE NEXT MORNING Linda and I looked like death warmed over. And to make matters worse, I grudgingly remembered my promise to bring Cougar back to the show. My sleep-deprived mind thought of walking him on a leash. It seemed only natural; after all, I was a dog person.

After showering more for comfort than cleanliness, it was on to toast for Linda, cereal for me, and more chicken for Cougar. Then we were off to get a collar and a leash. I walked the aisles of the store with Cougar in my arms, so we got the correct size—and found one blue like his eyes. Then we were off to the show.

After entering, I glanced nonchalantly at the Ferrari, then put Cougar down, held the leash, and followed. I didn't think about it then, but "exotic" no longer had to do with a special car—but a special cat. If that transition happened in just one miserable night's sleep, what more was in store for me? I noted that Cougar walked past the pet store display disinterestedly, just as I had the Ferrari. We both were changing. The assistant raced over, commented on how alert Cougar was, and remarked, with reservation, that all sales were final. She hesitated for a moment, then asked how I had trained him to walk on a leash so quickly. My answer was that I just gave him the opportunity to teach me.

Today was so different from yesterday! Today, he was visiting the show on his terms and the future would be the same. He walked, I followed. And when he got tired, I carried him until he wanted to walk again. Of course, I'd occasionally steer him one way or another, and it wasn't long before each of us could predict where the other one wanted to go. The next step would be discovering the whys. Yes, now he was cute and cuddly and I could pick him up, but those days were numbered. I always viewed him as an adult, not prompting any behavior that wouldn't be equally appealing after he had added two hundred pounds.

Before I knew it, it was dinnertime. Yes, there were laws against pets in restaurants, though I didn't consider Cougar a pet. So I selected an eatery owned by a friend—a small, quaint place dimly lit with candles, making one feel like Paris was on the other side of the door. Cougar snoozed (yes, he was winding down) in my lap until salmon was served. My plate hadn't hit the table before two paws were between the fork and spoon. The waiter winked and asked if he should bring another plate. I responded no, thank you, my hand would do. And it did, one bite for me and the rest for Cougar. Thankfully, Linda never ate more than half her meal, so the other half was mine. Then there was dessert. I had apple pie à la mode. At least I had apple pie; someone else licked the ice cream. Tomorrow, I would research what he really should eat. I was sure an occasional serving of salmon and ice cream wouldn't be harmful, but I wanted the best diet possible.

Because of our out-of-the-way table, only one couple discovered Cougar. They loved him. Given the circumstances, though, I felt it especially important to remain as inconspicuous as possible. I didn't want attention. During the drive home, I thought about this dinner and how it had set the stage.

I've always enjoyed living on the edge—the secret being timing and control. But to be accepted while doing so requires much, much more. People dislike what they don't understand. I knew I was doing something unique and should respect everyone's opinion, even if it was contrary to my own. I had to educate them while at the same time being respectful and courteous.

Some might suggest that I was just infatuated. So be it. Every minute of every day my feelings intensified and they would continue doing so. This relationship would reorder my priorities and change what I considered important. Through my feelings for Cougar, I would recognize the importance of being good neighbors with all wildlife. I wanted to teach people that mountain lions are to be respected, not feared. There are those who would disagree, selfishly continuing to degrade the environment. Then there are those who only claim to be sympathetic. A few owners of exotic animals are exemplary, as are some environmental agencies; but most are animal-dungeon keepers or fanatical, tax-exempt, self-proclaimed saviors, exploiting the very animals they claim to be saving. I don't wish to delve into their hypocrisy, their sham, their greed. I will only say it doesn't work for me.

My thoughts were interrupted when we pulled into the garage. As always, Chivas was prancing on the other side of the door, and I was sure Regal was there, too. I handed Cougar to Linda, opened the door, and trod into a tornado of slobber, nose, tail, and paw. Linda followed and, after taking several steps beyond the mêlée, set Cougar down. After I had "loved on" Chivas for several minutes, he turned and bounded toward Cougar, who just walked away. Chivas stopped and, oh so delicately, inched his nose under Cougar's tail. I'm sure Cougar found this a bit unsettling, but he continued walking. Chivas then turned and ran back for more human attention with an expression like: "Cats! Who needs 'em?" And from Cougar's perspective, it was probably the same regarding dogs.

I thought I could better keep track of Cougar by tethering him in the solarium–dining area with some twine. It wasn't long before his tether was wrapped around the legs of the dining room table and most of the chairs. Nothing novel, but what happened next truly was. Cougar, realizing that his travels were curtailed by seven or so encirclings, gently backed up until the line was taut. He then examined which way it was wound around a leg and proceeded to unwrap it by walking in the opposite direction. He continued to do this until he had the entire tether back. Wow!

I thought of the way people who keep wolves talk about how much smarter they are than dogs, and this made me think about the domestication process, all that selective breeding, and how it may have a negative effect on the animals' intelligence. If intelligence isn't what the breeders are seeking, then maybe, over the years, the ability to solve problems subtly erodes away.

Whatever the explanation, this mountain lion seemed smarter than his domesticated relatives. I wonder if the animal's intelligence makes training easier or more difficult. I guess I'll have to ask Cougar. He's the trainer.

THE PANELED SOLARIUM was to be his territory: wood-framed windows, a corduroy couch, a large-screen TV for him to watch nature films on, wooden chairs, and, of course, plants. Nothing, I thought, to really damage. Cougar immediately zeroed in on the couch. It was, after all, against the window where, just on the other side, birds bustled and squirrels scooted. And it was cat-comfortable. Unfortunately, there were two behaviors that added up to trouble. One, Cougar was teething. Two, he is a chewer. From his perspective the armrest was the perfect teething ring. So after he got comfortable and watched Bambi on TV, or the real thing through the window, it was chomping time. I thought turning the TV off might work, but the chewing continued. He just sat in the corner of the couch, got cozy, and started chewing. First the arm disappeared, then a cushion, then another, then the other arm, then the back. In two weeks, the couch, or what was left of it, looked like a buffalo carcass. Material was stripped from its wooden skeleton and metal springs were laid bare. When Cougar wasn't in the solarium–dining area he put his dental signature on several leather chairs and punctured a cushion of my wraparound living-room sofa.

Anyone who knew me and my obsession with physical possessions would have thought my relationship with Cougar was finished. Especially at a time when I was losing everything. I surely didn't want to accelerate the process. But maybe the loss

of my physical belongings forced me to cast off their importance. For whatever reason, I didn't just sit idly by as Cougar
destroyed the solarium. No way; with what little money I had
left, I bought him another couch. After all, there was nothing
comfortable to sit on in the solarium but bare springs. I was a
strict disciplinarian in rearing my two children. So what was
going on here? Was Cougar subtly demonstrating to me that
there's more than one side to everything? Was I now to go with
the flow, rather than bucking it? It sure didn't sound like me.

I've mentioned that Cougar was exceptionally intelligent. So
why didn't I just sit down and explain that chewing the furniture
was a no-no? And if he didn't listen, then why not punish him?
Well, punishment may appear to work, but with cats there's a
unique problem. Cats see it one way—theirs—which kind of
sounds like me in the years B.C. (Before Cougar). If I were the
spiritual type, I'd wonder if someone upstairs was getting even
with me. At any rate, cats are uncanny at accomplishing what
they want, but blind and deaf to anything contrary to their
wishes. Cougar figured out how to unwrap his tether because
he wanted to. When I scolded him after he chewed the couch,
from his perspective it was I who had lost his marbles. Cats are
not only able to survive on their own, they're good at it. Their
one-sided nature is well suited to surviving. For some groups of
felines, whether African lions, male cheetahs, or feral cats, survival depends on company, but that is unusual. Cats are self-
centered souls; what they want, they try to get—simple, end of
story. The secret is to make them want what we want and believe
it was their idea. Who knows, this approach might even work

for humans. But just because felines are considered aloof and distant, DON'T think for an instant they are.

Rescuing Cougar seemed only right, but understanding him and making him happy would have to follow. I could relate to his one-sided nature, but because of him I no longer thought one-sidedness was appropriate for me. How ironical . . . good for him . . . bad for me.

2

"HE'S MY BROTHER"

IT IS SAID that cats are independent and aloof. A mountain lion is a cat, and that makes me think. How do we really know what cats are like when we're thinking human? Their actions may *seem* independent and aloof, but are they really? I mean, when it's dinnertime or the cat-carrier comes out of the closet, cats are anything but distant and detached.

It appears that we are more like dogs, in-your-face social. But I believe cats are distant-social, can be mentally with us when they're across the room. They may have their eyes shut while sitting in the sun, but those ears are tracking our every move. If they were aloof, what we were doing wouldn't matter. So maybe cats embrace from a distance, unless something really gets their attention, like food or a threat.

Mountain lions are considered solitary, which is the wildlife professional's way of saying independent and aloof. But are they really that different from us? Mountain lions hunt more efficiently than any other cat, capturing prey 80 percent of the time as a solitary hunter. When it's off to work, they'd rather go alone. So how many of us take our spouse to work?

The male mountain lion has three or four females occupying his territory. Every so often there will be that siren scent wafting through the air, indicating that it's time for a romantic cruise. The male seeks out that particular female and mating occurs for a week or so; then he leaves. Of course, this has no human parallel.

When kittens are born, the mother raises them until they become adolescents, able to fend for themselves. No one knows why the family breaks up, but I believe it has to do with food. My theory is that the mother senses it's time for another romantic cruise, so it's time to get away from the kids. But they need a little push; consequently, she doesn't provide them with their usual free meal. After all, they all have become accomplished hunters. Thus the youngsters disband, looking for dinner; they set up their own territories and the entire process begins all over again. I repeat, any similarity to human behavior is purely coincidental.

Granted, the male doesn't return home every night, because he works on the road. Besides, his entire territory is his home. Of course, this behavior has no similarity to that of traveling salespeople, truckers, or military personnel. But don't think distance is being detached. Have an intruder visit his female, then check out the male's reaction. It's anything but indifferent. So I think it would be reasonable to say that the male remains in touch from afar, utilizing scent until it's time to cruise or his mate is threatened. Again, any similarity to our using telephones and letters to keep in touch is coincidental.

I know people who appear distant while living together. Why not cats? Hey, whatever floats your boat: Relationships can be spatially distant or close. Far be it from me to give advice or label someone's behavior solely on what works for me. What I do object to is someone believing that his way is the only way. Without realizing it, that's what we humans do in relation to animals. And when we label cats independent and aloof, we're comparing them to us. That's not fair. Their behavior may be different from ours but with similar emotions.

So the key, I believe, is being objectively perceptive. Observe what's happening and try to make sense of a behavior without human bias. This is tough, but absolutely necessary. When I observe Cougar objectively, what his world is like becomes increasingly evident.

I was committed (maybe a pun, maybe not) to understanding him, a cat that was gaining the weight of one house cat per month. I, an admitted dog person, had vowed to live—sans bars—with this little guy who was becoming bigger. My edge, if I had one, other than unwavering dedication, was being perceptive. So what were the odds? Was ignorance bliss? I would have to take it one step at a time—and the first step was housetraining.

Kitty litter seemed to be the logical solution; millions of house cats couldn't be wrong. So I poured some of Regal's litter into a reasonably sized box, placed the box in a conspicuous place, and waited. Cougar immediately caught my drift and approached, more out of curiosity than necessity. He then stepped into the sand and began to sniff. Wow! This was a piece of cake. I was quietly patting myself on the back when he started preparing the litter for business. A long and powerful swipe, then another, and another. From my vantage point his front paws looked like serving spoons as they scooped the litter over the sides and onto the carpet. The dust lingered, but I could see that most of the litter was now scattered on the carpet. He hesitated. Yes, I thought, this would still work. Trying to contain my enthusiasm, I then watched him step out of the box, sniff, and pee on the carpet. Well, at least he hit the litter.

Okay, okay, so my celebrations were a little premature. Recognizing that litter was out, I tried to think of an alternative. Then it hit me. What does everyone spread on the kitchen floor for kittens and puppies? Newspaper! I would later discover that the scent of wood was a key factor in this, but now I was just searching for answers. Besides, I was tossing newspapers in the trash every day. Now it's recycling! Cougar zeroed in on the beckoning scent of paper in the box, squatted, and . . . splat! He bombed Saddam Hussein smiling defiantly on the front page. But the bathroom situation wasn't solved that easily.

Cougar seemed to epitomize the saying, Out of sight, out of mind. If his box was near, there was no problem taking care of business. But if he was wandering about, which was most of the time, he would frequently make mistakes. Later, I would discover that my error was thinking human.

You see, humans locate their bathrooms by sight. I would learn that most of a cat's life is nose-driven. So placing Cougar's box by using my eyes didn't get it on two accounts. First, they were my eyes, not his; second, and much more important, the location didn't smell right. And when cats make bathroom mistakes, scolding them is like telling someone his religion is wrong. It's the same with cats. The secret is to understand their creed, grasp why they behave a certain way, and then go with the flow rather than against it. I had a lot to learn. I would discover that placing his box where he made a mistake—from a cat's perspective, where it should have been in the first place—worked every time. And by watching him sniff around when he was first becoming familiar with a room, I could locate the box in the correct place before a mistake was made.

And the plot thickens. The scents prompting urination and defecation are different. The scent for stimulating urination is urine. The scent to provoke pooping is something wet and musty. Unfortunately, my house had ideal places scattered all over: the heating/air-conditioning registers, which had a moist-musty scent. The heating and cooling process results in condensation, the moisture mixes with something in the ducting, and the perfect place to poop is created. Thinking this behavior was interestingly deplorable, I asked others with big cats, and in a whisper they all confessed to the same problem. Every single one.

The power of smell continued outdoors. Cougar would be walking, smell where an animal had peed, then promptly cover the pee with his own. With regard to the other end, Cougar sought dampness: the top stair of the swimming pool, the edge of a stream, or damp leaves. House cats, because of generations upon generations of selective breeding, may have had this response muted, but trust me, it's there.

RELATIONSHIPS ARE A little more complicated. What interested me greatly was that in nature Cougar would be living what we would call a solitary existence, keeping in touch by scenting. But with Chivas and Regal, Cougar was anything but distant. Eventually the three became brothers. When brothers are together at home, territorial squabbles abound. But when one of them is threatened by an outsider, it's a different story.

Regal was low man on the totem pole and scared of his own

shadow. Though initially he was larger than Cougar, within two weeks he wasn't. Regal and Cougar never squabbled, much less fought. Cougar was the undisputed cat king. They would occasionally share the best catnapping place—under the stereo cabinet—but if Cougar started to get playful, Regal would run.

Regal always read Cougar's body language and steered clear when necessary. Cats know cats, big or small. Dogs, however, speak a different dialect. A dog wags his tail when he's happy, but a swishing tail means business to a cat, whether it's attached to a cat or dog. No wonder Fido happily approaches Kitty for the first time wagging his tail, and is met with a hiss.

Chivas was a tail-wagging saint, had the patience of Jove and the power to swallow Cougar whole, but seldom objected to him. Chivas was eight years old when Cougar arrived; his rollicking puppy days had evolved into a dignified adulthood. His face and body now reflected the sedate silver of experience. Snoozing had become much more appealing than scampering. When he took the initiative to stroll around the house, Cougar's boundless kitten energy would inevitably stalk, leap, and grab Chivas by the ear. Beleaguered Chivas would look puzzled, with his newly acquired ear ornament hanging on for dear life. If I was nearby, Chivas would whimper a request that I remove the problem. But if alone, he would rub Cougar off on the carpet.

If Chivas was pushed, he'd snap back. But Cougar reacted to a snap with, "Okay, I'll leave, but don't expect me to stay away long." And Cougar's persistence was backed up by rapid growth. Indoors, he ruled the roost, where his size was daunting; but outside, his being bigger was better for everyone.

Regal was constantly harassed by the neighborhood dogs. He

reacted by meekly darting from bush to bush even in his own front yard. Then came a day in the early spring when, tempted by the premature seventy-degree weather, I decided to wash my car. Chivas remained inside, snoozing in front of the window on a beige carpet turned gray by his siestas. Hanging plants above him created shadows as the sun's rays soothed the aches of age. Occasionally he twitched and whimpered, chasing squirrels in his dreams. But the feline duo preferred adventure, and so Cougar and Regal stepped outside with me.

Regal immediately darted to the nearest bush for cover as Cougar was drawn to the undulating coils of the garden hose. Then, after five minutes or so, Regal uncharacteristically stepped out into the open to sun himself even though the neighbor's dog was sleeping on his porch across the street. This dog, unfortunately for Regal, was the most pugnacious in the neighborhood. He immediately saw Regal, sat up, and proclaimed his presence with a muffled yelp. This time, Regal didn't race for cover but instead actually lay down. I stared in disbelief, the garden hose splashing water against the side of the car.

The dog barked, sounding more forceful this time, and stood up. Regal just licked his paws. Was Regal nuts? This dog would grind him into hamburger. Then, out of the corner of my eye, I noticed Cougar crouched behind a bush. He was glued to the situation. The dog started to trot, then run toward Regal, letting out short trumpeting barks as his paws hit the ground. His nails clicked across concrete while Regal continued to clean himself. Cougar's rear end pitched back and forth as his tail, like a scythe, slashed grass up by its roots. The instant this dog invaded our territory, just twenty feet from Regal, Cougar exploded from behind the bush. The dog, with a high-pitched yelp, spun around faster than a top, his nails this time not strutting, but gouging the concrete in his race for home. Cougar, after his initial burst of speed, slowed to a lope that carried him past Regal and into the street as the dog dove through his screen door. Cougar paused, looked at the ragged hole in the screen, then turned around, walked up to Regal, bumped noses, lay down, and started cleaning his paws, too. This was immensely interesting to me. Granted, Cougar would protect his mate out in nature, but in this case he had protected another male cat, whom he had adopted. The surprises, however, didn't stop there.

It wasn't long before the word was out among the neighborhood animals: Don't mess with Regal. Regal now walked without fear. All the dogs gave him room, just in case Cougar was behind a bush. Regal even began to give Cougar a little of his own medicine by standing up to him. It was truly amazing. Regal was learning to be a lion.

Dogs are different. Characteristically, they're spatially less distant than cats. And nothing will get a dog's attention faster than protecting his territory. Chivas, on the other hand, would welcome a burglar to our home. Chivas never asked for trouble. Everyone, human or animal, was his friend, so fighting was unnecessary, that is, until one day when he, Cougar, Linda, and I spent a weekend visiting Indiana's Brown County, a place that boasted covered bridges with settings to match. If you stretched your imagination, you'd swear you had stepped back a century.

We were staying in a log cabin motel surrounded by expansive oak trees and an emerald green lawn, with cornfields and cow pastures in the distance. On our last day, as the early morning mist was dissipating, a one-horse Mormon carriage plodded by. I was packing the car for our trip home and thought Chivas would enjoy resting under a big oak tree about sixty feet from our front door. He seemed to be in seventh heaven as I tied him to the tree; from there he could watch us, enjoy the setting, and remain safe from occasional traffic. Several local dogs approached, wagging their tails, and Chivas greeted them.

After packing the car I returned to the room to leash Cougar, who at the time was one year old. He had been looking out the window and couldn't wait to get outside. He literally yanked me to the door. After I opened it, he quickly hooked to the left and streaked away, ripping his lead through my fingers like a band saw. A millisecond later I discovered the reason. A huge—I mean gigantic—German shepherd was barreling toward Chivas. His teeth were bared, he was snarling, and he was seconds away from an elderly golden retriever who could do nothing but accept the consequences.

I couldn't possibly have saved Chivas from this vicious attack, and still to this day I don't know what provoked it. I was powerless, but instinctively I ran as fast as I could. What could I do? Thankfully, Cougar was faster and stronger, and he did know what to do.

Cougar was flying. The German shepherd, this malicious overgrown meat-grinding canine, was approximately Cougar's size and was several feet from Chivas when, to me, everything went into slow motion. I could see viscous saliva streaming from the shepherd's exposed canines, his ears pointed, his eyes riveted on a meek Chivas, who just licked his lips. Just as the shepherd's head rotated to rip a section out of Chivas's throat, the sky over him darkened. Then came the hit. Cougar's front paws harpooned him, so hard that the shepherd's body rolled for what seemed an eternity—over and over, grass, dirt, and legs swirling in a cloud of dust. Cougar had delivered the energy of a hundred-pound weight hurtled at forty miles an hour. Then Cougar stood motionless, watching as the shepherd tumbled to a stop, faltered to his feet, wobbling at first, then limped away, then picked up speed and ran. He never looked back.

I surrounded Chivas with an embrace. Cougar watched, stepped closer, then bumped noses, first with Chivas, then with me. Compassion is complicated. There will be some who see the above happening as anything but empathy; to them, Cougar was just chasing a dog, period. So let's continue.

Spring in Indiana means thunderstorms. There's something about lightning and thunder that seems to terrify most cats and dogs. Several weeks after we returned from Brown County the skies opened up with a fury. Shock wave after shock wave of thunderous explosions shook everything. Cougar napped on the solarium floor with one eye open—not scared, just curious.

Before the storm, Cougar, Chivas, and Regal were all napping separately. Catnapping with Cougar was like sleeping with a time bomb. You never knew who was going to wake up first, and if it was Cougar, it was time to play. And when Cougar pounced, only he was having fun. But all this changed when someone needed help.

After the first thunderous pounding from the heavens, Regal approached Cougar, bumped noses, curled up, snuggled close to his chest, and went to sleep between mammoth forelegs and paws. Chivas was next. He ambled up, speared his nose under

Cougar's tummy, scooped underneath until Cougar's midsection was six inches in the air, lay down, and, though shivering, was still.

Cougar was a sight, like a hen guarding her chicks. He couldn't put his head down because Regal was there. And it must have been uncomfortable resting on Chivas's hard skull. But Cougar didn't move for forty-five minutes, until the storm had passed, at which time he quietly got up for a drink of water.

Cougar was the strength of the triad, but it was all for one and one for all. Several months later, after we'd visited friends and their baby boy, Cougar came down with a fever and upset stomach—the identical symptoms the baby had. Cougar glued himself to the floor and didn't move. Again, it was Regal who first approached, bumped noses, and curled up beside him. Then Chivas sauntered up, sniffed Cougar, and curled up on the other side. They spent all day beside Cougar, just getting up for water.

So animals may be emotional. But what about when cats bring home "presents"? Those poor little birds and mice. The cat sure didn't display emotion when these defenseless creatures fell to instinctive urges.

Does that mean cats are different from people? Last time I was eating dinner at a restaurant, I didn't see any somber faces when people were eating steak, lamb chops, or veal. Or is it okay when we have animals slaughtered for us, even their young, but it is instinctively cruel for a cat to sharpen its hunting prowess on an occasional mouse or bird? Hypocritical, I say—for all but vegetarians.

Diehards might argue that this was their dinner, but the cat was just having fun and didn't eat its prey. So am I to understand that people don't enjoy wearing leather belts and shoes or carrying a purse made from skin? How about a hat with feathers? Did anyone ask what happened to the bird? The excuse will be that since the bird is now dead, someone might as well enjoy the feathers. Humans can rationalize anything and find fault with everything; a person wearing a fur coat may argue that it's keeping him or her warm, and besides, no one complained when our ancestors had to do the same.

Look, I've eaten steak and encroached on our environment with the worst of them. But as I attempt to view the world through Cougar's eyes, it becomes increasingly difficult to sweep all these contradictions under the rug. Animals have almost a saintly character: they find fault with no one. My guess is that birds don't ridicule us for not being able to flap our arms and fly. And I'll bet porpoises don't make fun of us for swimming like anchors; instead, they help us. And cats don't mock us for not being able to catch mice with our bare hands. Just the opposite, in fact: they present them to us as gifts.

AMAZINGLY, THERE WAS another mountain lion living a mile from our home. John and Bev kept Getty, a 150-pound South American cougar, out back in a large cage attached to the house, occasionally allowing Getty to come inside. They had bottle-fed Getty two years before, and most would have considered their relationship with him quite close, like that of parents and child.

I invited John and Bev over for dinner, not only so that they could meet Cougar, but because I wanted to tap into their two years' experience with a mountain lion. That evening John observed Cougar and me. When Cougar wanted something he'd chirp. And if I didn't respond immediately, he'd grab the cuff of my pants and pull me. John mentioned how connected we were. Cougar was not only dependent, but trusted that I could and would help him. John also noticed that I stroked Cougar with the side of my face, and he wondered why.

It's all about human bias, I explained. We use our hands to pet, but I don't see cats doing it that way. When cats get close, they use the side of their face. My whiskers provided a tongue-like roughness to which, when I stroked his face, Cougar always responded with a thunderous purr. There have been times when I'd offer my hand and Cougar would turn away, wanting my face instead. I equate it to closeness. In human terms, sometimes a handshake is appropriate, but at other times only a kiss will do. It all boils down to bias. Get rid of human bias, objectively observe the actions of cats, then mimic them.

Some cat people might say that their cats don't want the side of their face, just a scratch or pat. Granted, relationships are complicated and diverse. Some people are tactile, whereas others don't wish to be touched; I'm sure cats are the same. But I have seldom seen a cat rub another cat behind the ear or pat with its paw. Paws seem to be more for playing. Caressing seems to always be accomplished with the face. I don't want Cougar to view me as a human outsider but as a cat in human clothing. Besides, I wasn't interested in an ordinary relationship; I wanted more.

While John and I were talking, Bev and Linda strolled by on their way to get a salad Bev had made for dinner. They opened the front door and walked to the car, leaving the door wide open. Cougar, who was between me and the door, watched the women go to the car; then he turned and bounded toward me. I had observed a similar behavior when we arrived at hotels. I would run to the room, open the door, and walk in; Linda would open the car door and Cougar would race ahead of her to the room. If she left the room, Cougar would remain even though the door stood open.

John asked if I was apprehensive that Cougar might get outside and I answered no. He asked why. I answered: Because I'm in here.

3

"NOISE, WATER, AND REFLECTION"

I TAKE COUGAR virtually everywhere. The day after he arrived home, Linda and I had dinner out while Cougar resided in my sweater with his nose poking out of the bottom of the V. There was never a "coming out" party for him. He was always out with people and extremely comfortable around them.

It was several months later, in early spring, when the three of us drove downtown to an outside event. We walked past a clown blowing up balloons for children. The hissing noise of the compressed helium was very frightening to Cougar. It's the only time I've seen him uncontrollable. He wouldn't settle down until we distanced ourselves from that noise. I assumed that it was like a sound he experienced while being shipped on the plane. And to this day he has been wary of clowns. After settling down, he rested in my arms, but most of the time he was down on all fours, crossing crowded streets and negotiating his passage through hordes of people.

I used to shop at the Fashion Mall, an upscale spot northeast of town, and Cougar would come along. There were many stores that looked forward to having him come in—the Sharper Image, a jeweler, a clothier, an art gallery. Then I'd walk over to the Radisson Hotel for lunch. They would seat Cougar and me, not in their dining room, but in a formal main lobby, like a sunken living room, with sofas, coffee tables, chairs, and someone playing the piano. Cougar would lounge on the carpet or sit on the couch while I had iced tea and a sandwich.

At six months of age Cougar weighed fifty pounds and pretty much walked everywhere we went. I needed to always know what he was observing, so walking out in front of him wasn't wise. Besides, walking in front of him meant being played with, whereas walking behind him meant that he was protecting me. Also, if he should happen to lunge forward when I was in front, it meant he got a running start of two leash lengths (twelve feet) before his leash snapped taut with the force of a fifty-pound weight going 30 mph. Consequently, a forty-five-degree cone behind him, on either side, became the optimum position. There I could watch him, either directly or indirectly, and should he lunge, I could swing from one side to the other, slowing him down and speeding me up in the process. Granted, I could observe him while walking directly behind, but that position didn't allow me to utilize his energy; if he lunged, I'd just be pulled over and land on my chin.

And what would cause him to lunge? It happens so infrequently, but once is one too many times if you're out in public and unprepared. Cougar might lunge at a squirrel, rabbit, or bird. He is occasionally interested in a dog on a leash, but never to the point of lunging. And he'll never lunge at a person, though he is always interested in little kids screaming and rolling on the ground. And I have to be especially cautious around stray cats. If one bolts, Cougar will, too.

So my knowing Cougar and being able to control him at all times meant we continued to go everywhere together. And

I never allowed anyone to pet him unless he wanted to be touched.

Almost every day I took him to a park. I'd attach his leash, get out of the car, and start walking. When approaching a tree or brush, he'd walk on the same side as I, so as not to tangle the lead. We would stroll to where there were few people and then I'd let him go. Sometimes he'd rush away and hide, stalk me, and jump out of the bushes. I knew he was out there . . . somewhere. At other times I would follow him and observe. If something was furry, fast, and close, he'd react instantly and try to catch it. When the potential prey was larger and more distant, he took more time. With a deer, he became very calculative. And he'd notice but always steer clear of snakes. For hours I watched and observed. If the day was warm, he'd be aware of the ground temperature and lie down when the soil was cool. Out there, I was the one learning.

Both in nature and in civilization his actions were the same. For example, he would establish or dissolve attention by shaking his head. Maybe this is comparable to humans trying to clear their head by shaking it. Obviously, it was important for me to recognize what was causing his adjustment. And as with all cats, a swishing tail meant attention, but the tip of Cougar's tail fluttering told me he was just noticing. Cats, big and small, have the same body language.

But two age-old cat clichés—the curious cat and the scaredy-cat—bothered me. They seemed to be describing two different animals. How, over the years, could cats stand for both? It made me think. Cats indeed are inherently curious, but not instinctively fearful, too. They, like Cougar in the plane, learn to fear.

Cougar has associated a hissing noise with the terrifying experience of being crated and taken from his family, but many fears aren't learned through a specific experience. Most cats are restricted to a house or an apartment. It is my belief that all animals, including humans, fear the unknown. So if cats, or people, are confined, they aren't comfortable with what's beyond those walls. Take human prisoners, for example: some "long-termers" even wish to remain locked up for fear of the chaotic world beyond their bars. I believe that when cats are confined in a house or an apartment, the same is true. If a cat has not experienced being outdoors—walking on a leash or riding in a car or boat—then many of these things can cause apprehension. Of course, it is almost impossible for a cat to take a walk in New York City; in such situations, providing mental stimulation becomes extremely creative.

Cats have become the most popular pet mainly because they're easy. Most will say that they just don't have time for pets. Okay, let's briefly list, in order of time spent, the three factors taking your time: job, family, and pets. Now let's identify, in order, who will always be there for you. Interestingly, the list has been inverted! It's a matter of the squeaky wheel getting the attention. Ironically, spending more time with pets lowers blood pressure brought on by spending too much time elsewhere.

Let's consider trust. Without it, whoever is presenting something new can't be relied on. When your cat becomes a flurry of fur, this might be the problem. Trusting keeps apprehension to a minimum. From day one, I wanted to share everything with Cougar and keep his new experiences as positive as possible. I was learning what he liked, what he disliked, and why. By presenting experiences to him systematically, I kept him interested and was able to observe. Before I did anything, I considered how it might affect him. Pretty soon I would have enough information to know what he wanted. One thing I learned was that going more than one hundred miles an hour on a boat was something he'd do just for me.

FOR SPEED NUTS, going fast means separating the needs from the wants. Speed is sometimes necessary in boating, but more often it's just an extravagance the go-fast recreational boater craves. It was because of this craving that there was an annual boat race sponsored by Shooters 21 Night Club/Restaurant on Lake of the Ozarks, located west of St. Louis and southeast of Kansas City. This was an opportunity for Linda and me to have fun and expand Cougar's horizons.

My boat was being trailered from Kissimmee, Florida, as Linda, Cougar, and I departed from Indiana in Linda's Jaguar. It was cool when we stopped for dinner. And because I always want to get where I'm going quickly, I parked in the restaurant parking lot, cracked the windows, and hurried to join Linda inside for a bite to eat. Taking Cougar in would have created a time-consuming avalanche of questions, but leaving him back in the car wasn't a good idea, either.

Cougar was frustrated. How come we got out and left him in the car? He took his frustrations out on the Jag. Cougar, being nine months old, now had adult teeth, and the Jaguar's interior was covered in hide. Upon our return, the headrests, the front and lumbar portions of all the seats, and the leather-covered handholds were peeled like bananas. Cougar just gave me a chirp, like, "Back so soon?"

I was still gritting my teeth when we pulled into the Lake of the Ozarks Holiday Inn late that evening. It was located next to the marina where the boat would arrive the next day. After confirming that pets were welcome (I failed to reveal the exact size), I checked in and quickly escorted my "pet" to the room. Hotel rooms for Cougar are new territories to explore, providing many glorious scents of former guests and their pets.

All three of us were tired as dogs—well, two of us were. The next morning I placed Cougar in the car with the air conditioner blasting and went back to retrieve Linda, who was lingering in front of the mirror with her brush. Cougar didn't mind being left alone in the car when I'd run a quick errand. In those cases, I would either park under a tree and crack the windows, or lock the car and leave the engine running with the cool air squalling. (In the latter case, I would always point the car into the wind, so that any exhaust fumes would blow clear of the vehicle.) But I never took Cougar in Linda's car, which was where he waited now. And, unfortunately, while I was back in the room, Cougar made a discovery. When he stepped on the center console of the Jag, the electric windows opened. After he'd mashed the switch and leapt, our secret was out. A cart being pushed by a housekeeper was captivating, so he followed immediately behind, swatting at the wheels. From inside the room I heard a yelp, kind of a cross between a scream and a yell, but I thought little of it.

I would be told later that Cougar quickly lost interest in the cart after its pusher vanished around the corner. A white miniature poodle hysterically yapping inside his owner's car seemed just as interesting. I was told that Cougar strolled over to the pooch's white Cadillac container, stood up, and placed his paws on the side window—and the poodle went berserk. Cougar watched as this barking bundle of energy ricocheted off the inside of the car like a golf ball in a shower stall. The car's owners, an elderly couple, opened their room door to investigate.

After I'd separated Linda from her brush and we'd both stepped outside, we saw the couple standing motionless, jaws agape, and realized the reason. I said good morning, strolled over to Cougar, hooked my finger around his collar, tugged lightly, smiled as if this happened every day, walked to the Jag, opened the door, directed Cougar to the back, raised the window, and motioned Linda to take a peeled seat up front. As we were pulling away, I saw the housekeeper, with company, hysterically pointing to her cart. Maybe they'll think it was a wildlife cat visiting from the surrounding woodlands, I speculated.

After a breakfast when no coffee was necessary, we drove back past the seemingly quiet inn to the marina. My boat had just arrived. I sped down to the parking lot, hastily bid Linda and Cougar farewell, and dashed for the dock. Cougar would have nosed around for twenty minutes checking all the new scents, so I asked Linda to follow me with him. After all, she'd always taken Cougar on his leash. But you know how kids grow; it seemed like only yesterday that he was just a kitten. However, not only was he approaching one hundred pounds, but he didn't want to be left behind. And I didn't just saunter away. I ran.

Between the parking lot and the water was a well-manicured carpet of grass sloping ever so slightly down to the dock. Cougar was riveted in my direction as Linda attached his lead and beckoned him to follow. And he did, quickly. Linda dug in, but it was no use. The lead was looped around her wrist, so instead of the leash snapping out of her hand, she was pulled and had to start running to keep up, which was not a good idea—it was the difference between 10 and 50 mph. She kept up for about two steps, then flew forward, hitting the lawn spread-eagled, and skipped along the grass like a surfboarder. Ahead was a three-foot stone wall. Cougar went up and over. Linda didn't. Luckily for her, Cougar stopped on the other side and chirped, request-ing that she pick up the pace a little. By then Linda's bright yellow outfit was streaked with green.

Her plight did not go unnoticed. Inside, the marina recep-tionist shouted at a salesman to go out and help. The salesman looked at Cougar and declined. So much for chivalry. But Linda didn't need any help. She possessed enough embarrassment to level the scales and began reciting to Cougar, who sat motion-lessly, all the reasons why it wasn't a good idea to drag her across the grass like an extreme sport act.

One thing had become crystal clear: it was the last time Linda would walk Cougar. But something more important had hap-pened. Cougar now knew he was stronger and Linda recognized she was weaker. This meant their relationship had switched. A house cat knows we are bigger and we stay that way, so our dominance remains intact. But Cougar was a tad different, grow-ing bigger every day. He was approaching Linda's size, and be-cause of today's happening he knew he could pull her off her feet and haul her, wherever he wanted to go accelerating all the way. He was bigger than her and Linda agreed.

Cougar minded his manners the rest of the way to the dock and rubbed noses with me as I asked him if he had been a good boy. He assured me that he had. The rest of the morning was spent flying low over the water in my boat and selecting the correct props for the upcoming race. Now, I'm not saying that Cougar loved skipping over the water at more than 110 mph, but he accepted it. As I saw it, I didn't much care for crawling on my hands and knees through sticker bushes, either. He was learning my side and I was learning his. When we returned to the marina, the dock looked pretty inviting to him, so he leapt to it as soon as he could, but he got a gold star for putting up with the wind and noise. We spent the rest of the afternoon with marina personnel. Cougar strolled into the cool and quiet conference room, decided this was more like it, and curled up for a nap. Whenever someone came in, Cougar would just open one eye, take a peek, and close his eye again. Pretty soon he'd have them feeding him and bringing water. One thing, though, never changed: no one offered to walk him. He had them where he wanted, and even became their official mascot. So who's the trainer?

Poor kitty, they said, he needs a quieter, more comfortable boat to take him to dinner. They offered to lend him a twenty-six-foot pleasure craft and even suggested a place where the locals hang out. So Cougar, Linda, and I drove back to our room to clean up.

Unfortunately, the message light was flashing. It was no surprise: I was told we'd have to leave. It was the first and last time that I'd be evicted from a hotel, and I can't say that I blame them. It was totally my fault. I called the marina for accommodation suggestions, and they told me of a Swiss-chalet-style motel on a bluff overlooking the lake. We checked out of the inn and into the chalet, showered, and were back at the marina, where three of our local friends were waiting to join us for dinner. After boarding Cougar's loaner, we were off.

The restaurant, a renovated fifty-year-old home nestled back in a heavily wooded inlet, was elegant in an informal way. After mooring at a moss-laden dock, our people party, plus one feline, followed the pier to a walkway that snaked around several trees to the front door. I walked up to the hostess and asked if they served exotic cats and she responded that, no, fish was their speciality. She then looked down and realized her mistake. Without further ado, and just as if big cats were forever welcome, we were shown to a large table in what used to be a living room. We were on the second round of drinks after ordering dinner when an embarrassed waitress approached to announce that Cougar couldn't remain in the restaurant.

Now stop for a moment and think what has happened. A cat has ridden in a boat, walked on a leash to a strange restaurant, waited patiently to be seated, walked to our table, then curled up by my chair surrounded by movement and boisterous noise. Why? Trust. Do animal relationships belong solely at home if opportunities exist to bring them along on outings? Of course not. Bring your animals with you. They need a change, too.

Not wanting to admit defeat, I asked if we could dine outside on the porch. The waitress vanished and quickly reappeared with a nod and a smile. I will always wonder if the approval had to do with our having ordered five dinners. I got up and Cougar immediately did the same. We walked to our table outside, which turned out to be much nicer, with cool breezes and quiet. Cougar curled up in the corner of the porch and I positioned my seat to block him in and any inquisitive bystander out. I am so proud when Cougar can come into a human environment and remain for hours and no one knows. The many people who came in after us and were seated on the porch had no idea that Cougar, who just snoozed quietly on the floor, was there, too.

But someone did notice. Halfway through a most delicious meal, I was suddenly forced headfirst into my plate by someone trying to rush past. I immediately shoved my chair back, preventing a three-hundred-plus-pound, unshaven drunken thug from getting to Cougar. I stood up and spun around. He was double my girth. He demanded to "pet the cat" and I responded that I didn't allow petting. He ordered me to move aside, and he stumbled away only after my six-foot-six friend removed his watch and joined me. Our waitress shyly and apologetically explained that this was the restaurant's manager. I couldn't believe my ears as I watched him stagger down the patio and into the bar. He was joined by several of his buddies, all laughing and slamming down drinks as if Prohibition started tomorrow. During the entire episode Cougar just rotated off his side and sat upright, staring at this intruder, like a machine gun on ready.

Under the circumstances, enjoying a leisurely dinner was impossible, so we paid our bill, left a generous tip because it wasn't our waitress's fault, and asked how we might leave without passing the manager. Unfortunately, there wasn't a way. So we got up, walked down the porch, and turned into the bar. As I was passing the manager, he pushed away from the bar and grumbled an expletive. His friends smirked their approval, goading him on. Cougar had had enough. He took two steps in front of me and hissed. The manager made a shrieking noise, as if he were gasping for air. Cougar answered with a snarl. The manager's face lost all color. You could have heard a pin drop as I turned Cougar toward the door and we departed.

Have you ever been humiliated? I wanted to tie Cougar to a tree, have Linda remain by his side, return with my big friend, and break a bar stool over this guy's head. I walked silently, listening to the others in the group express their disgust, attempting to stay calm, trying to talk myself into just walking away. When we got to the boat, Cougar immediately jumped in and used his tray. Consternation always affects him that way. When he really gets upset, his bowels go into hyperdrive— which gave me an idea. We had walked past the manager's boat, a hot pink cigarette boat with the restaurant's logo along the side. A lightbulb lit up deep within my evil mind. Cougar had finished, but I hadn't. I scooped up what he'd deposited on the newspaper, and while the manager and his cronies watched from the window, I walked over to his boat and dumped Cougar's gift on his seat. I then returned to our boat and we drove away. There, now Cougar and I both felt better.

THE FOLLOWING MORNING was race day. Shooters was the center of attraction. Radio and television bellowed their live coverage over a newly constructed fancy facility with picture windows, mirrors, live band, plush carpeting, inside dining, outside snacking, and a dock that looked more like a marina. Cougar, Linda, our three friends and I skipped over the water from the marina to Shooters. As we approached, Cougar was on the bow, like a hood ornament, anticipating getting off. There had been a contest for the best-decorated boat and the judges were still in place with their three-by-four-foot grading cards. As my engines belched our arrival, the line of judges waved their cards—all 10s. We had won first prize, but I wasn't there to go slow.

While I was away racing, Cougar would be comfortable at Shooters in a nice lounging area, where he could remain calm, cool, and collected as he rested on a designer carpet in front of the window, watching the race. Linda was there, too. The loud race coverage was turned off in that area and soft music took its place. I had a waiter instructed to hand-feed Cougar ice every ten minutes or so until I returned.

After winning the race and accepting the trophy, I returned to Shooters. Carman, the owner, suggested that Linda, Cougar, and I stay for dinner. What a difference a day makes, compared to the night before: vaulted ceilings with huge cathedral windows brought the ambience of the marina and lake inside, joining long narrow candles, linen tablecloths, silver settings, and a New York menu. Cougar, as always, curled up next to my chair.

And especially since this was elegant dining, did anyone object to Cougar? As a matter of fact, there was one table that did. They were politely invited to leave, but they elected to stay. After watching Cougar for most of their dinner, they began to smile, and then to laugh as he occasionally stuck out his paw to trip waitresses walking by. (The restaurant personnel, well aware of this mischievous kitty-cat, kept their distance from the table when carrying trays.) When the former anti-Cougar folks finished dinner, they came over to commend us on how well trained he was. I thanked them and explained that, actually, it was he who was the trainer. They looked down at a plate that had held steamed shrimp and agreed.

After dessert there was dancing and more for Cougar to discover. Just downstairs was a gigantic mirrored disco with a multifaceted suspended sphere that rotated, hurling reflected laser lances through the darkness. Up seemed down and right appeared left as Cougar chased specks of light to the thumping of disco rhythm. It was surreal.

Because the dance floor was extremely dark, illuminated only by occasional shafts of intense light, amazingly, there were a few dancers who didn't see Cougar chasing specks of light around their legs. Allowing Cougar to experience different happenings always attracts attention, but it was extraordinary for him to be able to do so unnoticed, which is my choice. This way he could sample without being sampled. If you think about it, everywhere a big cat goes, he creates attention. Out in nature, when he is near, birds squawk, squirrels scamper up trees, racoons freeze, deer dash. So when he's in civilization and gets an eagle eye, nothing has changed.

WE LEFT THAT night for home and stopped at an interstate hotel, just wanting cleanliness and a good night's sleep. I was asleep before my head hit the pillow and Linda fell asleep almost as quickly. Unfortunately, the air conditioner broke as we slept and the room got warmer and warmer; too warm for Cougar. When we awoke the next morning the room looked like the roof had been destroyed off by a twister where everything inside had been sucked up and come crashing down. Cougar, how could you? I pleaded. The mattress of the other bed was against the far wall, the upholstered chair was on its side, the lamps were unplugged and overturned, and the telephone cord was chewed in two.

Cougar was uncomfortably warm and I didn't awaken to his request to rectify the problem. As we tried to correct the catastrophe, it made me reflect.

Yes, I wanted to share the world, both civilized and not, with Cougar. And yes, I was already being told that our relationship was without equal. But if Cougar was going to mingle and get close to society, then I would have to get with the program, mentally be ahead of him. He was, after all, a big cat—not mean, not wild, but big. What would have happened if that little white dog had gotten out of his car? Absolutely nothing, but do I want to take the chance? And what was I going to do about the telephone, the broken lamp, and the rip in the mattress? I realized that being with Cougar means zero tolerance. For his sake and others', I could never take chances.

In the past, advice came fast and furious. Get your life back after losing your business, get a job; then, and only then, spend time with Cougar. After all, helping, observing, and learning from an animal is beneath you and won't put food on the table. My friends would have applauded had I announced that I was finding a "nice home" for Cougar—as if sweeping him under the rug—but in so doing I'd abandon not only Cougar, but myself.

There are dreamers and those who make dreams happen. My dream is that Cougar be happy and well adjusted. And as an ambassador for wildlife cats, he can help people get up close to a mountain lion, realize through him how special his cousins are, and understand that we can safely coexist with them in nature. And let's not forget his little house cat relatives, who deserve our understanding, relating, and caring. But I'm not going to accomplish any of this with my head up-and-locked, as it was that weekend.

Others, in their own way, are well-meaning but misdirected. I'm talking about some animal rights organizations that fanatically lash out at those who show animals and place them in competition. I believe animal abuse is everywhere and maybe competition encourages some people to push their animals, but there is probably no other group in which people spend hours every day with their animals, training them. Is it less abusive to allow your pets to stagnate mentally, spending fifty minutes of quality time with them a week, if they're lucky? Look, everyone has the right to his or her opinion, but frequently the answer lies somewhere in the middle and we'll never reach a compromise by using terror. Yelling, screaming, and threatening get attention, but not respect. And for lasting positive change to happen, people have to feel that it's right. Fortunately, most of the environmentalist camp is made up of well-intentioned, dedicated souls. I wanted to join them.

It has always been my belief that we can't help anyone without first knowing the person we're trying to assist; otherwise, we are only serving ourselves—doing what makes us happy. Idealistically, we might say we can best help wildlife cats by allowing them to live without us, but that's just not going to happen. In fact, we are encroaching at an alarming rate. They have no place to go. Building a home or camping on their turf, is like being neighbors. So why not know thy neighbor? To help wildlife cats, we have to know them. And we can't totally understand them just by observing them in cages. Behavior is complicated.

Just a seemingly unimposing photographer in Zimbabwe sitting at the wheel of his jeep taking pictures of cheetahs creates a change in their behavior. The photographer informs us that his pictures are of cheetahs living in the wild, unaffected by humans. These cats, however, use his jeep to shade themselves from the sun, then maybe get a higher vantage point atop the hood to observe potential prey. So we're all connected; it's just a matter of scale.

I'm not advocating ownership of exotic animals. That demands total dedication, sacrifice, concentration, and a life-style change few will commit to. But I couldn't allow Cougar to be abused, either, to become another big-cat statistic—born in a cage and destined to die there, too. So I'm devoted to turning a negative into a positive by applying all the firsthand behavioral knowledge I gain through him, helping all cats, big and small.

With regard to big cats, they are creatures of habit, choosing to take a path, rather than not. Crossing an open field, they will hopscotch from shrub to tree, seeking cover. They inevitably prefer walking *along* something, like a hedgerow or fence. And even if a fence is only five feet tall, they need to be motivated to hurdle it; they prefer walking beside it.

Where a highway intersects big cats' territory, knowledge of their habits can be used in providing a way for them to cross safely. A wildlife tunnel under the highway should be constructed, using a known deer path. If deer are then herded through it, the cats will be right behind. Some say bridges are better, but without cover, the wildlife cats and I'd guess the other animals, too, will avoid it like the plague.

Tracks can be revealing. When a large cat is walking, the only paw print you observe is that of the rear foot, because the front paw searches for the best spot to step, for quiet traversing, and the rear foot follows right on top. And tracks don't mean just paw prints on the ground. Take grass, for an example: cats love eating a special wide-bladed crabgrass and they leave a signature when they shear it with their teeth—a characteristic edge that looks like a mountain ridge. When searching for big cats, I inspect the kind of grass Cougar eats every day.

None of this knowledge is out of books—it has come from Cougar. I have inherited him, his family's and his relatives' cause. If there's a way it is non-biased perceptiveness, looking at the world through wildlife cats' eyes. Well-intentioned animal people *must* overlook human bias and attempt to take the cats' perspective; if they did they'd truly be helping. But how can they relate to wildlife cats? Studying wildlife cats on their own turf, really getting close to them, contradicts the very reason people are on safaris: to observe wildlife cats without affecting their behavior. But we have to get close to truly understand these animals. From afar, we can only guess. There seems to be a contradiction. And wildlife cats living in a human environment normally provoke skepticism, because most exotic cats are there for all the wrong reasons. Hopefully, Cougar and I are different. So it seemed only natural for me to take the first step toward well-intentioned people who many would consider to be my most vociferous critics—animal rights and environmental organizations. Ironically, they have become my staunchest allies.

I first called Elizabeth Saxton at Defenders of Wildlife. Our rapport was instant, and I was able to assist her on several projects. Eventually Cougar was featured by the Endangered Species Coalition, made up of the top three hundred environmental and animal rights organizations worldwide, at their conference in St. Petersburg, Florida, October 1–2, 1994. Then Suellen Lowry from the Sierra Club invited Cougar to an executive strategy meeting in St. Pete. All lovely, well-intentioned, educated people, who have listened to Cougar.

4

ARE CATS REALLY

INDEPENDENT AND ALOOF?

MY GOAL IS to know. In relation to human beings Cougar was anything but independent and aloof. When it came to Chivas and Regal, he was actually protective and watchful. Some might say that animals have a way with one another, but not with humans. Which is my point exactly: The problem is us and our interpretation of them. I believe cats are dependent and close but just show it differently. Each day, Cougar and I have become more dependent on each other—in his way and mine.

There are days, however, when he needs correction. And after I discipline him, he becomes extremely close to me, but only if the disciplining is insulated with times of being close. If I punish him repeatedly without giving some form of praise, after a day he begins to lose that extra-special closeness. And how do I scold a mountain lion? For small corrections, I just raise my voice. Cougar knows I am upset, and normally that is enough. But if a greater correction is needed, I not only raise my voice but put him in "time out" after swatting his behind. Rejection and then isolation is the ultimate punishment. And the old cliché, it hurts me more, is certainly applicable. We had an upcoming trip in September 1992, where I would pay particular attention to our mutual dependence and closeness and how it allowed us to do the things we do.

Packing for Cougar immediately reveals our dependence on each other. He paces right behind me as I pack his food, his cooler (because he likes crunching ice), a bowl from an admirer for ice water, a three-foot rawhide bone for his pearly whites, and a dozen or so empty plastic liter bottles that when he chews them, by their crackling noise, signal that he is hungry. Both the plastic bottles and the rawhide bones would be eliminated from future trip lists because of their potential hazard. There is also his "litter" box, a two-by-three-foot forest green plastic tray designed as a park for puppies to use as their bathroom, absorbent medical pad liners because newspapers weren't absorbent enough, and an assortment of plastic bags, paper towels, and baby wipes for cleaning up. But the two most important things to pack are . . .

Winkle, a fuzzy brown toy Bullwinkle moose. Winkle was purchased when Cougar was twelve weeks old, and Cougar immediately had a wildlife crush. When sleepy or just for calming, Cougar will grab Winkle by his bulbous nose and fall asleep looking into those shiny button eyes. Other stuffed animals are ripped apart and scattered throughout the home territory, but Winkle remains, to this day, no worse for wear, sometimes requiring surgery and an occasional rhinoplasty, utilizing my athletic sock as an implant. Separation occurs only when Winkle hits the washing machine; then Cougar curls up like a croissant by the dryer door. We've searched far and wide for another Winkle, as backup and eventual replacement, to no avail.

Next is an infant-receiving blanket named Nursey and/or

Blankie. As a cub, Cougar started with a pink blanket. He would bury his head in the fluffy folds and suck on the thick satin piping. Then, when we were returning from the Florida Keys, somewhere approaching mid-state, it was discovered that Nursey had been left behind. After Linda and I argued about who was at fault, I pulled into a Kmart as Cougar napped in the car. I thought pink was too feminine for a boy and one blanket wasn't enough, so we walked out with yellow Nursey II and powder blue Nursey III.

THIS TIME WE were packing because of a phone call asking what were we doing on Labor Day weekend. It was the 1992 Miller Genuine Draft Virginia Beach Offshore Grand Prix III inviting Cougar to be their mascot, along with sports celebrities Pete Rose and Joe Theismann. We were invited to participate in a world-class sporting event on the beach, have a chance to catch up with my old powerboat racing buddies, observe the East Coast Volleyball Championship, join a marlin fishing tournament, and enjoy a one-of-a-kind fireworks display, all expenses paid.

But where would we stay? I had learned an Ozark lesson or two. Normally, when traveling in the car, we'd just stop for the evening, requesting a ground floor room close to the parking lot. We were in, slept, and away before anyone knew Cougar was there. And the room was always left in perfect order—another Ozark lesson. But at times, during trips, I had to work at remaining inconspicuous, as when we'd be offered a second-floor oceanfront room. I'd make up a story that Linda had a broken leg, only to be told that the elevator was close to the room. I'd answer that Linda was claustrophobic, only to be told we couldn't see the water from the street side. I'd answer that Linda hates the water. So then, with expressions of sympathy, I would finally get a remote first-floor room overlooking the parking lot. They never found out about Cougar. But sneaking Cougar back and forth from the room at Virginia Beach during the entire weekend's festivities was close to impossible. Besides, he was the star.

The Tropicana Resort, a seven-story beachfront hotel on the boardwalk, was right on the start/finish line and was the center of attraction. What better place for Cougar to stay? Over the phone I could tell that their manager, Ana, was intelligent, professional, understanding, and, most important, an animal person. So when I told her that Cougar was the mascot for the upcoming event, she was honored and offered a first-floor oceanfront room on the other side of the parking lot. This time I accepted. I really prefer water to concrete.

It was 2 A.M. when we rolled into the Tropicana's parking lot. We checked in and collapsed into bed. But not before putting Cougar's uneaten food and water into the small refrigerator under the counter.

It was several hours later, when my eyelids felt like anchors, that I was awakened by a commotion. Cougar was hungry and had crunched on his plastic liter bottle until it looked like soggy toast. So, in frustration, he took matters into his own paws by opening the fridge door, scooting a bowl of food off the shelf, nosing it across the floor, and knocking it into the wall, gouging food out with his tongue all the way. After dragging myself out of bed, I hand-fed him, put ice into his water bowl, arranged

Blankie and Winkle, and collapsed back into bed. The last thing I remember was Cougar licking himself, cleaning up.

Thankfully, Cougar's first appearance the following day was not until a dinner reception at the Clarion Beach Hotel for the three hundred drivers, owners, mechanics, and crew. Race officials were to introduce Joe Theismann, grand marshal for the weekend, and celebrity driver Pete Rose; thus we had most of the day just to relax. Early in the morning, Linda and I jogged on the beach while Cougar snoozed in sixty-eight-degree comfort. Cougar likes it cooler than seventy-four degrees—seventy five or warmer and he's uncomfortable. Unfortunately, the rising sun reflecting off the surf must have increased the room temperature to an uncomfortable level. Whenever Cougar is bothered or wants something, he comes to me, a dependence thing. I can even prepare his food on the kitchen counter, turn around, leave it, and walk away and he will follow, leaving his food on the counter. When I'm not around, he will not ask Linda for anything, but just wait till I return. In this case, since I wasn't there to adjust the room temperature, he decided to improvise. He yanked the mattress off the bed, dragged it over to the refrigerator, opened the door, and lay down to snooze in comfort. When Linda and I returned he chirped as if he didn't need anything. I was impressed that, in lieu of knowing how to use a thermostat, he connected a soft mattress and cool temperature, making himself comfortable.

That evening the race reception at the Clarion was taking place in the hotel's ballroom overlooking the ocean. Linda, Cougar, and I entered through ten-foot solid oak doors and were immediately surrounded by the crowd. It is feline nature to be apprehensive, but Cougar *trusted* me that it was okay. The buffet table didn't get a rise out of Cougar. No shrimp, thank God. Then one of the race officials escorted us to the head table.

When people view Cougar, acting doglike, entering a large room full of people, they don't seem to realize just how special that is. Inevitably someone will ask if Cougar does any tricks. I answer that the trick is for *them* to experience, enjoy, and learn from him. Actually, I believe doing "tricks" would be counter-productive. I want people to realize that mountain lions are intelligent and compassionate. I believe tricks are degrading and focus attention on the trick rather than the magnificence of the creature. Cougar stands alone, representing his wildlife cousins, and tricks aren't necessary.

AT THE HEAD table, we were pleasantly interrupted. "Jesus! Now that's a cat!" came from behind me, with an accent more Chicago than southern. I turned to see a deeply tanned man in his early forties, with receding curly black hair, a black mustache, a muscular build, and a gold chain that was buried deep in chest hair. His gleaming eyes and smile made him instantly likable. He wore shorts and a light blue polo official's shirt with the name "Bob" embroidered over the pocket. "Hi, I'm Bob Veith," he said, extending his hand with a smile. He then extended the back of his hand for Cougar to sniff. He was doing everything right. At first he was standing up, just bent over slightly, offering the back of his hand. In a flash, watching Cougar, I had to make a decision: Do I allow a close encounter or not? It's all a matter of Cougar's focus. A woman at the time of her period will cause too much focus. With Bob, Cougar was perfect: interested in Bob, but not too much so.

"Have you been with mountain lions before?" I asked.

"No, but I've always admired them. Look at him. He's unbelievable."

After introductions, Cougar lay down and Bob sat down next to him. They were nose to nose when Cougar put out his front paw to steady Bob's face, then started licking those curly black locks in long continuous strokes from eyebrows to crown. There's something appealing to Cougar about the smell of hair cream. I tugged lightly at Cougar's lead, but Bob waved me aside, saying, "This is great. Someone get a camera." I knew Cougar could pull hair out by the roots with his tongue, and Bob didn't have much to spare, but he would willingly have accepted baldness for the experience. Cougar continued grooming until Bob's curls were slicked straight back.

"That's awesome. Now I'd better get this show on the road," Bob said, getting up, turning toward the podium, and adjusting the microphone. "Why don't you and Cougar sit in front of the table so everyone can see him."

Gosh, this guy's important, I thought. But it wasn't until several weeks later that a thank-you note from Bob on race stationery revealed that he, in fact, was Commodore of the Grand Prix.

"Ladies and gentlemen, may I have your attention."

As Bob spoke, Cougar felt an air-conditioned breeze; it caused him to plop down on the carpet of abstract palm leaves in shades of pink and green against a gray background. A green table skirt dressed the speakers' table behind us and a pink skirt draped the riser on which the table sat. The surrounding pastels made Cougar's golden eyes and tawny fur jump out, as if from the undergrowth. Pete Rose came through the double doors wearing an emerald green exercise suit, and silently waved to the crowd. Nobody noticed . . . all eyes were on Cougar.

Then Cougar's tail began to swing like a pendulum and he began looking around. He was bored. I tossed him a stern look. He looked away and stared at the pink riser skirt. Cougar, basically, likes attention, and at this point all eyes were on Bob. Cougar gently batted the skirt with one paw. It moved! He swatted it harder, for confirmation. There was a rustle of whispers. All eyes turned to him and he knew it.

Let's not forget how independent and aloof cats are supposed to be, especially in a strange setting. Cougar wanted the attention of the crowd and being aloof wasn't the way to get it. Bob announced that there were several modifications to the rules list, but no one seemed to care. Then Cougar grabbed the riser hem in his teeth and yanked. Thumbtacks securing the riser snapped off in rapid succession like distant machine-gun fire, tacks ricocheting off the carpet, bouncing, and spinning to a stop. The audience suppressed its laughter. Bob continued as if nothing had happened. To my horror, I realized that those tacks might look like bugs to Cougar. So without hesitating, I attempted to gather them up.

Now, since I consider myself calm under fire, I thought it would be appropriate if I began reattaching the skirt as if nothing had happened. Cougar watched my every move. I pushed the last thumbtack into place and settled back next to Cougar, who was watching the crowd intently. Then he slowly stretched his head back, grabbed the hem with his teeth, and ripped the skirt away again—pop . . . pop . . . pop . . . pop—just as before. This time the audience exploded into laughter.

Bob peered down from the podium. I froze as Cougar looked at the audience, as if asking for encouragement. Then Bob continued to speak. This was ridiculous; I had to get control. I scraped the tacks into a pile, scooped them up, and hurriedly tossed them under the riser. Cougar was acting just like a little kid, knowing full well that he could act up without being scolded because he had an audience—an audience that was goading him on. Does this sound independent and aloof?

My tossing the tacks under the riser, thinking out of sight was out of mind, didn't work. Cougar was totally into the game. He stood, walked over to the only skirt that was still attached, and yanked it off the riser.

Now everyone was howling. This wasn't like a ball or toy I could take away and hide in the closet. I had to restore some semblance of dignity to the situation, but tacks were everywhere. I rolled the detached skirt up into a ball, gathered the tacks, and threw everything under the riser. I then gave Cougar my most parental stare. He avoided my glance and looked at the audience for support.

"Now it's past time to introduce the Miller Genuine Draft Grand Prix mascot," Bob announced. "This is Cougar—and David Raber." I smiled, rose to my knees, and nodded as Cougar glanced back and forth between the audience and the riser.

After the applause, Bob continued, with a grin, "Cougar has also been appointed our Chief Complaint Officer. So all complaints, both before and during the race, should be presented directly to him. Once again, welcome to Virginia Beach. Together we can make this the best Grand Prix ever. Good racing! Meeting adjourned."

As Cougar was being surrounded by an invigorated crowd, it occurred to me that he had become just like me. I occasionally enjoy being a ham; it's like an exclamation mark at the end of a sentence. But most of the time I savor solitude, being by myself or with someone special. So, to, with Cougar. After mingling, there will be a time when he's had enough, and he'll get up and walk away. He'll want to grab Winkle by the nose and curl up with Blankie. I can be next to him or across the room, but I have to be there. That night, after around an hour of being with the crowd, he got up and tugged me toward the door. I knew it was time.

THE NEXT MORNING Linda and I went for our jog. Before leaving Cougar, I pulled the drapes shut to keep the room cool, piled his water bowl Mount Everest high with ice, set the thermostat on Antarctica, got Winkle and Blankie together on the bed, and slapped the "Pet in Room" sign on the door. "We'll be right back. We love you," I said, closing the door behind us.

Running on the boardwalk was great. It seemed that most of Virginia Beach was either walking, running, Rollerblading, cycling, or just gazing at the ocean. Dolphins swam parallel to the beach; waves crashed like distant thunder, then receded with a hiss like morning bacon sizzling in a pan. Life was good, but something was missing, so I turned around after only a mile and ran at a faster pace back to the room. In the distance, a crowd of twenty or so people came into view. The closer I got, the more I worried. My fears became reality when I discovered that they were outside our window.

Cougar apparently got bored, so he yanked the curtains open to watch the boardwalk activity. Then, after taking in the crowd, he jumped back on the bed for a nap. I looked over the shoulder of a young boy of about twelve and peered inside. He exclaimed, "Hey, there's a tiger in that room."

"Nah," I answered, "tigers have stripes; besides, that's my room and I'd know it."

"What's on the bed?"

"That's my suitcase."

"Well, your suitcase moves and has two ears and a tail!"

"Hmm," I murmured, taking Linda by the arm, walking around to the front door, and going to our room.

"This isn't going to work," I stated, closing the drapes, to the disappointment of an ever-growing crowd.

"How about safety pins?" she suggested.

I knew that wouldn't do. Most cats curl up on windowsills the way plants turn toward the sun. But with Cougar, it was simply wanting to know what was going on. Besides, he knew the window was there; he'd either duck his head under the drapes or rip the curtain rod off the wall. And I didn't like pins.

I decided to ponder the question in the shower while Linda got an iron from the front desk. While I was sudsing, Cougar opened the drapes. An elderly couple was standing outside the window in hopes of seeing Cougar. The man had propped his bicycle against the side of the building, and she, a woman of about eighty, wearing a black and fluorescent pink spandex riding outfit with matching crash helmet, gently elbowed her way to the front, cupped her hands over dark glasses, leaned against the window, and peered inside.

At that moment I walked from the bathroom with a towel. Cougar stretched his head back over his shoulder, with an expression like, "Don't worry, they're looking at me."

After I was dressed, Linda came back with Ana. "Ana has a solution for crowd control," she said.

"Really?" (hoping it wasn't eviction).

Ana began: "Security says there has been a crowd outside your window all morning. And the local media called the front desk, asking if we could let them into your room for pictures. Follow me, I've got the answer."

Not to be left behind this time, Cougar ran for the door. Independent and aloof?

The three of us followed Ana to the elevator and she pushed the up button. Ana was twenty-eight, tall and slender, with brown eyes and long dark brown hair that bounced on her shoulders when she walked. Even though she worked with vacationers, she was fair-skinned. She probably thought the beach was frivolous, being more comfortable behind a desk or solving problems. She was the perfect hotel manager.

I watched Cougar sniff the floor and commented that other animals had used the elevator. Ana smirked. "Dogs maybe, but no lions."

The elevator crawled up to the seventh floor. When the doors opened Ana crossed the hall to an entrance, inserted a special key, and threw open the door. "Welcome to the penthouse," she said. "The owner would like you to be his guests for the duration of the Grand Prix. We think you'll be more comfortable and safer here than on ground level."

To the right was a master suite with a king-size bed, mirrored wall, and bathroom with sunken tub. In front of us was the living/reception room, with picture windows, marble fireplace, wet bar, sofas, tables, and chairs.

"Ana," I gasped, "you didn't have to do this for us."

"I didn't," Ana answered almost dryly. "This is Cougar's suite; you will be staying next door. He needs room to move around Follow me to the servants' quarters."

To the left she opened an adjoining door to reveal a large bedroom suite complete with kitchen and fireplace.

I took Cougar off his lead, allowing him to explore the entire territory as Ana bid us farewell, saying housekeeping would bring up our things. I could get used to this.

"David!" Linda yelled. Linda was behind the bar, gesturing for help. Whenever Linda hides behind the furniture, it's a sure sign that Cougar is roughhousing. Dogs wag their tails, dance, or spin around in front of you to show enthusiasm. Cougar likes to stalk and to swish his tail, which can be intimidating, even if he is just playing. Cougar was hiding behind a chair, head motionless, low to the floor, hindquarters dancing side to side in a rapid jig as his tail beat lint from the carpet.

"Cougar," I yelled, a fraction of a second too late as he sprang toward Linda from behind the chair and landed on the sofa, where I tackled him, both of us rolling up and over the back and dropping to the floor with a thud. If I hadn't intervened, he would have jumped from the sofa to Linda, head-bumped her or stood up on his rear legs and leaned on her shoulders as part of the game. It was part enthusiasm and part dominance, like saying, "I'm excited about this new room and I'm still the boss." Interestingly, this playful behavior never happens when Cougar and Linda are alone. He wants to reestablish the hierarchy when we are all present. Does this sound independent and aloof?

The parade was next on the agenda: race boats gleaming and dignitaries waving as they made their way down Atlantic Avenue. But unfortunately a misty drizzle didn't cooperate. Some felt it necessary to carry umbrellas, while others just turned up their collars. A year before, a good-natured old man had teased Cougar, then a kitten, by scratching the point of his umbrella on the floor, then hiding it behind his back. I requested that he not tease Cougar, but the damage had been done. It took all of five seconds. Cougar will now seek and destroy umbrellas wherever they are—under taxi drivers' seats, behind the doors of car salesmen, on display in a store, at the concierge desk. I've lost count.

Cougar, Linda, and I had just been introduced to the mayor—a delightful lady—when it was time for the parade to begin. Cougar was supposed to ride on the deck of a trailered race boat with all the race officials immediately following the mayor's car. To the side, we passed a policewoman leaning on her umbrella. Umbrellas were a dime a dozen given the inclement weather, but most were open. This particular umbrella, however, was rolled up, just like the one used to tease him. As we walked by, Cougar grabbed the umbrella and continued walking as if nothing had happened. The policewoman stumbled, and after taking several quick steps and regaining her balance, was face to face with Cougar, so it was only natural for her to reach out for her umbrella. Cougar just stared and bit down, hard. The shaft cracked like a twig.

"It's just misting; he can have it," she said with a smile. "My present."

After a thank you and a smile of appreciation for her understanding, we were beside our parade race boat on its trailer—with yet another problem. The deck was fifteen feet in the air. The race officials had gotten into the boat with the aid of a boarding platform back at the staging area, but we'd been too busy talking with the crowd. Now, with all the parade participants taking their proper positions in line, there was nothing but a rope ladder, which was difficult for Linda to climb and much more so for Cougar. At the prearranged time, the mayor's car began rolling down the parade route. There was no time; our boat had to move or block the entire parade. But I had an idea. I would coax the umbrella out of Cougar's mouth—which isn't all that easy. It's a matter of getting his attention away from the umbrella. I put my hand on the end of the umbrella, then made a loud hissing noise, then another. Cougar suddenly released the umbrella, because hissing is feline for "Back off!" It always works.

But Cougar still had his eyes glued to the umbrella. Just underneath the bow, I bent down, then sprang up, releasing the umbrella and arching it back over my shoulder toward the deck. Cougar leaped fifteen feet straight up, landed, and caught the umbrella before it hit the deck. I could have practiced that throw a thousand times and not improved it. I motioned Linda up the wobbly ladder and followed as the boat slowly began to roll down Atlantic Avenue, to the applause of the crowd, amazed that it's easy to get a mountain lion onto a slippery fiberglass boat deck surrounded by thousands of excited people if you know how.

From our vantage point, we parted a five-mile, tumultuous sea of people. And because of the mist along the parade route the crowd wildly applauded Cougar, seeing him on the deck with an umbrella in his mouth, as if he knew umbrellas were appropriate for this type of weather. I admit Cougar doesn't use an umbrella in inclement weather, but he's smart enough to always know where one is, and he's also smart enough to come in out of the rain. If it starts to pour, he will seek shelter, then lick himself dry.

The following day, Sunday, was race day. I watched from the balcony as crews readied their craft. I was jealous. God, I wished I were down there. The excitement of being on the edge in competition! Some day . . . maybe I would strap in again.

The phone rang. It was Ana, wanting to know if I would play host to a race party. The owner of the hotel wanted to use our suite for a dignitary reception and, of course, everyone wanted to meet Cougar. I said sure, knowing full well that watching the race was over.

Unfortunately, everyone seems to think that coming over to Cougar's place would be so easy for me, but they are mistaken. Nothing could be further from the truth. At home or in a hotel room, Cougar and I are surrounded by guests and in tighter quarters, plus we're in his territory. It's anything but comfortable and much more demanding than being onstage, because I have zero tolerance. If he just stares at someone, making him or her feel uncomfortable, I have failed.

It's a matter of control. One should never ever relinquish

control, especially with a large cat. Life just presents too many variables. I would learn that when we are onstage everything looks easy because we are in control. Cougar is in front of me not only because everyone wants to see him, but because I am able to look through him to the audience. If something gets his attention, I know about it. When I'm in control, I'm comfortable.

The waiters were knocking on the door before I hung up. In the back of Cougar's suite they set up a large buffet complete with meat on silver trays, cheeses, salads, fruit, and hors d'oeuvres. In Cougar's honor, Ana had supplied a huge crystal bowl of shrimp. The bar was fully stocked; the bartender polished glasses and started slicing lemons and limes. An hour before race time the room was packed with men in blazers, women in brightly colored cruisewear, and children decked out in expensive summer attire.

"Hey, David, where's Cougar?" It was Bob Veith with his infectious smile, his black curls glistening, awaiting Cougar the beautician.

"He's resting in the other bedroom," I answered. But before Bob could respond, a middle-aged woman wedged herself through the crowd.

"And this is Margaret," Bob announced. "I've been telling her all about Cougar and she wants to meet him."

At that moment, a man wearing a Grand Prix blazer just like Bob's approached, carrying a portable phone. He whispered something in Bob's ear.

"Excuse me, I'll be back," Bob said, grabbing the phone and commencing a conversation as he walked away, leaving me with Margaret.

Margaret was probably in her late fifties, but looked older, with her black hair pulled tightly back into a bun, and her gaunt cheeks scarcely supporting fifties-style glasses. She had skin so fair it made talcum look tan. Her outfit of lavenders and browns hung on her frail body as though they'd been put out to dry.

"Where's Cougar?" she asked, with a little-girl giggle.

"He's in the other bedroom, napping," I said, feeling a little bit like a tape recorder.

"Did I tell you about my dog dying?" she offered. She didn't wait for my answer. "It was in the car on the way to Hilton Head. They say that it either was a heart attack or my mother squashed his head in the car seat. Anyway, he was dead, so I covered him with mother's blanket until we could get to a gas station."

"Hmm," I responded, not knowing whether to react with sadness or a smile. I desperately needed someone to save me, and caught sight of the knockout punch. What Margaret lacked, this woman had. Nature had endowed my savior with all the necessary rope to throw me a line. She could have sat on her dog's head and I would have forgiven her, maybe even traded places with the dog. This was a woman men rush to. The kind some married men start conversations with at the drop of a hat, slipping their wedding band off and putting it in their pocket: five-foot-eleven, three quarters in legs and the other quarter in bronzed cleavage. Her green eyes were so alluring they held your gaze up, forcing peripheral vision to take in all the rest.

"Hi, are you Cougar's dad?" she asked in a voice so low it sounded as if it came from her knees.

"Yes," I answered as I was bumped from behind.

"And I'm his mother," Linda said, stepping to my side just as this lady's distinctive perfume settled over us like a sheet. The woman winked and uttered in a hushed tone, "We must get together sometime." Then she walked past.

"Looks like she's been out all night in that dress."

"Uh-huh," I answered, watching her bare back disappear into the crowd.

"I mean, sequins and heels! Like she's advertising!"

"Uh-huh."

A little boy tugged on my Dockers. "How about Cougar?" He was around six, with round bronzed cheeks, dimples, and blue eyes. His yellow polo shirt and his suspenders adorned with sailboats proclaimed that he was to enter a life of private schools and stiff upper lips. "Where is he?" he asked with a slight lisp.

Unfortunately, children and mountain lions don't mix. It's no one's fault, really, just that children see lions as toys and lions have the same opinion of kids. Kids do all the wrong things, like scream and roll on the ground. And even if they stood up, they'd be on the same level as the lion. Children lack all the powers of adults standing tall and staring.

"He's sleeping," I answered, "but I'm going to see if he's awake. Maybe he can come out now."

"Gee, really," the little boy shouted, his eyes bigger than saucers.

"You bet." I began mentally to prepare. If only I could control several of the unruly kids set adrift by their parents. There are always a few around—children whose parents believe it is every-one else's responsibility to baby-sit. Without them, Cougar could roam unattended.

I excused myself, walked toward the "Servants' Quarters," where Cougar waited, opened the door, and was met by a resounding chirp. I had waited too long. I bent down for several minutes of rubbing and scratching, attached his lead, and walked him back to the party. Within seconds no one cared about the race. Cougar's nose immediately tilted high into the air. Shrimp! Ana did say that the shrimp were for Cougar. Right? Cougar was focused on shrimp and I scanned the entire room. With this type of focus, Cougar could safely run through a daycare center. I released him from his lead and instructed everyone to stand still for a moment. Actually, focus is more powerful than a leash. He followed his nose as if on rails, crouched, popped up, and landed on the buffet table—two front paws at the base of the bowl, one back leg between the cheese plate and the croissants, and the right rear paw slightly displaced outward, just missing the butter. A lady named Ginger picked up her plate, not the least bit startled, saying, "My cat loves shrimp, too."

With a quick flip of his tail, Cougar turned in my direction, making sure he wasn't in trouble; then, hearing no rebuke, he lowered his head into the bowl. There was silence, then laughter as he came up for air. Several pounds of giant gumbo later he raised his head and licked his chops. Since focus was disappearing as quickly as shrimp, I was beside him. When he was ready to jump off the table, I quickly attached his lead and followed him. Ginger continued to inspect the buffet, forked a piece of roast beef, looked into the empty bowl, and announced, "We're out of shrimp!"

I heard race boats in the distance, screaming a high-pitched whine as propellers broke the surface, casting sheets of water into the air. But my attention had to be focused elsewhere. When racing, the crew has to remain focused, and when walking Cougar in a room filled with people, many of whom are drinking, so do I.

When you are walking a dog, you can take a mental break. But with Cougar it's all concentration. It's more mentally draining for me than landing on an aircraft carrier. Even when Cougar stops, I can't let my guard down. I can even tell you what leg he is going to start walking with regardless of his stance when he stopped. I discovered that his front legs are pushed by the rear ones. So if he stops with his two front legs together and his right rear leg is forward, which incidentally is a common cat position, then he will lead with his right front foot. When the left rear leg is forward, then the left front foot will move next. Is this important? Probably not, but I want to know everything.

The afternoon consisted of answering questions and explaining what mountain lions are like. It would only be later that evening, watching the extravagant fireworks, that we finally could relax. Thankfully, this display was just outside our balcony—solitude as Sunday's sun sank into cool Atlantic waters with high thin cirrus suspended like steam.

Pink turned to magneta, to lavender, to gray, then to darkness. We waited on the balcony, listening to the drone of people below and the pop of firecrackers, until it was time. Cougar recognized the thump of the fireworks cannon sounding like an underwater explosion and watched the fuse as it climbed higher and higher, his excitement soaring right along with it, until finally the blast came and the entire sky came alive with color and motion, expanding like an infant universe, with planets shooting out . . . arching down . . . blinking . . . flickering . . . and then were gone.

I didn't see it directly, but watched Cougar, his wide eyes reflecting the cataclysmic display. Then darkness, when his tail stood still, twitching at the end, wanting it to happen again; then thump went the cannon again and the faint spark of the fuse spinning wildly as it climbed, his head tracking the exact position of the projectile soaring higher, anticipating. Then, finally, a shock from the heavens, when everything shudders and the next spectacular display expands into a kaleidoscope of color.

I love it when Cougar's happy, because we're dependent on each other and close—two human traits considered human and not normally associated with felines, but it's what makes us special. So how do I get close to Cougar? Could it be the little things, like always hand-feeding him, or putting ice in his water bowl, or brushing him when he wants it, or cooing to him dozens of times a day, or turning down the stereo, or living with plastic covered couches and chairs, or letting him inspect everything brought home, or always making sure that he's comfortable, or constantly moving Nursey and Blankie to his current resting place, or always dropping what I'm doing to feed him, clean his tray, put more ice in his bowl, or scratch his chin? Or maybe it's the more general things, like doing nothing without first considering its effect on him (Cougar is always first), or sharing my life with him, twenty-four hours a day. It's probably not any one thing, but all of them put together—because as soon as I feel it's not important to fulfill just one little duty, then not putting him first is just around the corner. It's a state of mind, a way of life, a mindset.

And to those humans-first-to-the-exclusion-of-animals types, let me say that just as calisthenics strengthens your muscles and reading exercises your mind, so does the act of giving make you whole. In the years B.C., I would consider my three worst faults as being egocentric, materialistic, and unable to forgive. Cougar has eliminated the first two. That wasn't why I rescued him; it just happened that way. And I'm convinced that our closeness sets us apart, just as closeness rockets teams in front of their competitors.

IT WAS CLOSENESS that made Cougar special in Virginia Beach and several years later it would temporarily place him in the international spotlight. No doubt you've heard of Puma, the international company making shoes and sportswear. Well, in 1995 Linford Christie, a 1992 Olympic gold medalist for Britain and considered by many the fastest man in the world, and Clinton Jackson, the U.S. Olympic high-hurdler, represented Puma. I received a phone call from Max Kraus, a soft-spoken California film producer who was directing a photo shoot with both athletes for Puma's summer catalog and upcoming European television commercial. A California contact of his had instructed him that, physically and mentally, Cougar was the best of the best and a great Puma's puma. Was this the right telephone number?

The next weekend, on Saturday morning, Cougar, Linda, and I followed Max's directions to a St. Petersburg film studio. I left Cougar and Linda in the car and went inside to check in. I was

astonished, realizing that beautiful promotional material originated from such clutter: spotlights dangled from poles, loose
wire was strewn everywhere, and the floor was covered with
what seemed like a decade of dust and debris.

Max approached, beaming from ear to ear. He was tall, hefty,
and exquisitely polite. He introduced me to the members of the
film crew who had flown in from Austria the evening before:
Harold, the head cameraman, who wore his camera around his
neck; the video man, David; and their assistant, Manny. They
all wore sunglasses with small round lenses; were quiet, courteous, softspoken, unbothered, and polite; and conversed in their
native German language, but switched to English, out of courtesy, whenever I approached.

Nadine was an Austrian model, just sixteen, with jeans pulled
over a sheer one-piece bathing suit and sunglasses nestled on
top of her long brown hair. Nadine breathed life into her bathing suit, and it was the plan that pictures would be taken of her
and Cougar until Linford and Clinton arrived.

Three brilliant white lights casting no shadows illuminated a
fifteen-by-fifteen-foot staging area located against the wall of a
windowless studio jam-packed with props and photographic par-
aphernalia in the surrounding darkness, where imagination
could go wild on a stormy night. A half-dozen silhouettes, Puma
executives and advertising people, were sitting on boxes and
folding chairs, ready for the photo session to begin. Nadine
slipped her jeans off and stepped into the light. I led Cougar
onstage. "Shush, Cougar is on the set," a loud whisper wafted
from the periphery as Harold quietly began giving directions to
Nadine. Cougar was on his leash; I instructed him to sit down

as I watched the cameras and tried to stay out of the picture. Harold instructed Nadine to kneel next to Cougar. The photo session had begun. Nadine immediately pushed closer and Cougar's whiskers snapped forward. I told her that she should back up, but she pushed closer. Cougar's whiskers remained forward, his pupils started to dilate, and he shifted his weight to one side. A paw was about to be launched her way, in a fraction of a second. I tugged lightly on his leash and his playful swing missed its mark. Nadine wasn't at all frightened, not even apprehensive—just felt rejected. She rocked back on her ankles and pouted: Why doesn't Cougar like me? I was pondering the same question.

Harold motioned for a short break. There was one question that I had to ask and diplomacy was impossible. Was it that time of the month? But Nadine said no. Okay, if that wasn't it, what was? Everything happens for a reason. I dislike it when people label, saying, for example, that Cougar's swat was his wildness. I'd prefer to understand the real reason. Besides, people calling an animal wild is like the pot calling the kettle black. As I was trying to figure out the answer, Nadine and Manny embraced in the shadows. There was my answer! I had suspected it before. There is a lingering scent after physical intimacy and Cougar can detect it.

I needed to take Cougar for a short car ride to clear the air. Max nodded okay. When we returned, most everyone was huddled around Linford, Clinton, and their girlfriends. Nadine broke away, walked up to me, and asked how she could be more appealing to Cougar. Unfortunately, that was the problem; she already was too much so.

Max intuitively shifted gears to Clinton. Clinton is an African American with a boyish face and a lean muscular build. He was to wear a swimsuit for pictures with Cougar. I positioned Cougar on his side and instructed Clinton to kneel behind him. The cameras started flashing. I then motioned Clinton to inch closer. Pop, pop, pop . . . the flashes made his advance seem like a twitchy slow-motion movie.

Clinton was relaxed, Cougar was calm, and the audience got into it by shouting, "Here kitty, here kitty," which at first irritated me. In retrospect, though, a slight distraction for Cougar was probably useful. Then, completely impromptu, Clinton knelt down and caressed Cougar's face. Harold and David swarmed in closer for tight shots. As I focused on Cougar for the slightest hint of irritation, I couldn't help but be impressed by Harold and David in my peripheral vision. They were everywhere, but never in each other's picture, working together— back, close, above, straight ahead, to the side, below—in cool concentration. They were totally absorbed in what they were doing, never mind that Cougar was a two-hundred-pound cat; they were too busy to be bothered. And their mental "distance" was calming for Cougar. He never once glanced in their direction.

It was going so well that Clinton decided to show off by sticking out his chin—like, "Give it your best shot, Cougar." He was behind Cougar, so he felt reasonably sure that Cougar couldn't see him as the cameras filmed from the front. The cameras clicked away. Clinton extended his chin further, daring Cougar to take a swing. Cougar didn't turn around, blink, or even flick an ear, but with lightning speed swung his paw up and around, catching Clinton firmly on the tip of his chin. Cougar's paw was back on the floor before Clinton knew what had hit him. "He never turned around," Clinton declared, holding his jaw, to the laughter of the crowd. Clinton then dropped to the mat, faking a knockout punch, yelling, "Cougar, you are the man." Cougar just gazed forward. He knew.

Everyone was laughing except one man—Linford. Lin, as his friends call him, is a black man from a large family in London. Lin seldom smiles. He is a grandfather and an Olympic runner. But all the speed he was capable of didn't make him comfortable with Cougar, and Clinton's mischief didn't help. Unknown to everyone was the fact that Lin had been bitten by a dog when he was three and had been afraid of dogs and cats ever since—never mind mountain lions. I tried to reassure him, saying that I would be close. Lin looked at me sideways and asked how much I weighed. He then asked how much stronger a cat was, pound for pound, than a man. I said that knowledge makes the difference. He wasn't impressed. All the sponsorship money in the world wouldn't make him get cozy with a mountain lion.

His filming, like Clinton's, started with him positioned behind Cougar. And like Clinton, Lin was dressed in a swimsuit. But all the coaxing from Harold, David, and the audience couldn't compress, squeeze, cram, or cajole Lin any closer. His fear was real; that dog had changed his life, and Clinton's session with Cougar had magnified it. From Lin's perspective, he was way too close already. So the rest of the day saw pictures being taken of Cougar, with Clinton up close and smiling and Lin distant and frowning.

———

I'M SURE EVERYONE secretly hoped Sunday would be better. It would take place not in the studio but on the beach at an exclusive St. Petersburg resort. Pulling up, I could see hotel guests having morning pastries and coffee on the porch. Ladies' bonnets rippled in the refreshing breeze. The beach in front of the resort was distinguished by heavy wooden lounges, each with its own umbrella, but all castles out here were made of sand. This was tourist season and the beaches were overrun by those not as financially fortunate, with their Frisbees and footballs.

The Puma entourage was assembling, enjoying the sand, seagulls, surf, and sun. Linda and I have a saying: Your worst day in Florida is still better than your best day in Indiana. There's something intoxicating about sunshine and salt water by a palm tree.

Beach attire is normally casual: shorts, cutoffs, bathing suits, and T-shirts. But when Lin and Clinton discarded everyday sweat clothes, revealing flashy beachwear, heads turned. A trampoline was positioned in the sand and the two world-class competitors were invited to have a go at it. Max wanted airborne shots, athletes in the air, though Lin was uneasy. Training on his level is so precise that he didn't want to risk spraining his ankle doing something different.

After several minutes of Lin, Clinton, and Nadine modeling active wear, a small crowd had gathered, but most beachgoers continued punching volleyballs, flinging Frisbees, and batting beach balls. After an hour or so, Max was satisfied with what he had and nodded that it was time for Cougar.

Cougar had been observing from his air-conditioned car and was excited about the trampoline. Those athletes bouncing high into the air really turned him on. As I was walking back to get him, Max explained to Lin that he wanted him to jog down the beach holding Cougar's leash. Lin just stared at him and strode off. This was supposed to be the scene in the television commercial, the main event, the primary reason we all were here and why an entire Austrian film crew was flown to the United States. And Lin was the main man, the fastest man in the world, the feature attraction. No one could take his place.

I could see Max's disappointment all the way from the parking lot as he waved me to come back alone. He explained the dilemma and was somewhat surprised that I agreed, in part, with Lin. I explained that cats don't run for fun; they have to be motivated. It wouldn't be wise to place a stimulated cat next to someone who is terrified. Lin's one-of-a-kind style would be all but destroyed by fear. And Cougar's form would be negatively affected by being close to someone he wasn't comfortable with. Besides, I felt that a leash projected the wrong message. I didn't want to promote exotic-animal ownership. Max just kept nodding in dismay.

But I had an idea. Why not have Lin run the beach by himself? Do what he does so well. Then have Cougar do the same. Then take Lin's footprints and graceful form, and with computer imagery, transform them into paw prints and Puma's puma.

If Max could have kissed me, he would have. But then a daunted expression crossed his face. "How is Cougar going to run a beach loaded with tourists?"

"Not a problem," I answered.

"Really?" Max exclaimed, half excited, half wishful.

What I had in mind was infinitely safer than Cougar on a

leash with Lin, which I wouldn't have allowed anyway. There are only several cats in the country trained to run for food. The same cats are seen in all the motion pictures requiring action shots of big cats. They are kept semihungry when a certain behavior is desired, are brought to the set in a cage, and are trained to run from that cage to another cage that has food in it. Unfortunately, though, if things don't go as planned, you have a large, hungry cat on your hands. If we were filming this by the books, a remote beach would have been selected; a ten-foot-high fence with a four-foot, forty-five degree inward-angle overhang erected; and seconds employed to stand in for tourists. A "trained" cat would have been brought in a week earlier and allowed to get comfortable running from cage to cage for food. But Cougar is different. He runs because he wants to, not because he's hungry. I'm not sure if Cougar has ever been hungry. Psychologically, it's completely different, requiring no "training," just being dependent and close.

But we weren't home yet. Lin didn't want to run in the sand. Again, it was radically different from his training. Indeed, the sand, for him, must feel like a swamp, tugging tendons and straining muscles. But alas, given the alternative, he agreed. A forty-yard section of beach in front of the resort was selected. Harold, David, and several other camerapeople got into position paralleling the water. Then Lin sprinted. His running looked as though he snatched his feet from the suction of the sand and kept them suspended for hours.

After several takes, it was time for Cougar. It seemed simple enough, having a big cat run along the beach, like, "Hey Fido, fetch." But this was a mountain lion without any practice or training. For perspective, take your house cat to the beach and try it.

I laugh when "experts" instruct how to train cats by using food. The truth of the matter is that most cats train us. There are several rules to remember. One, go with the flow, utilizing their behavior. Two, have a close, trusting relationship. And three, look at the world through their eyes. Bias is our worst enemy.

Most people would be inclined to say they have a close relationship with their cat. Let's see. Does the cat come when you call? And I don't mean just when you have food. Does the cat always communicate with you? Is the cat miserable when you leave? Is the cat at the door when you return? After returning, do you stop what you're doing and offer the cat a sniff of you and anything you are carrying in? (Cougar always sniffs my mouth if I've been out to eat.) Do you share every possible experience? Is the cat frightened of riding in the car? Do you feed the cat by hand? Does the cat respect that there are certain times when you are not to be disturbed? Do you realize that everything you do affects the cat?

Besides their seemingly autonomous nature, one reason cats are so popular is that keeping them is pretty much effortless; relationship is on easy. Just put a bowl of water down, fill the food dish, clean the litter box when it reeks, and occasionally scratch them behind the ears. They, after all, supposedly enjoy being distant. But remember, differing personalities aside, you act the way you're treated.

So, back on the beach, it was time for Cougar to apply what I have proclaimed and make history. Time to erase the notion that food is the only thing cats understand. Time to establish that trust trumps training, that knowledge defeats ignorance, and that love conquers all. Cougar, Linda, and I walked to the edge of the beach, just short of where the sand was packed solid by the surf. Harold, David, and the other camerapeople were waving—they were ready. Even Max was in position with his Instamatic. The seagulls and surf were doing what they have done for millions of years. And people were doing what they have done for hundreds of years. But this day was different.

I handed Cougar's leash to Linda and she dug her shoes into the sand. I glanced at Cougar, blinked softly, turned around, and slowly walked away. Behind me, I could hear Linda asking for help in restraining him. I peered over my shoulder, making sure Cougar was secure, then turned and ran. I could feel his presence. He was with me. After forty yards I stopped, spun around, locked onto his stare, and fell to my knees. Linda and her helper couldn't have restrained him any longer if they'd tried.

He lashed at the sand. Within several strides he was traveling faster than a dune buggy, adroitly darting back and forth, missing anyone or anything in his path. An elderly couple walking the beach never saw him as he streaked between them at more than 40 mph. Then he hurtled over a Frisbee skimming the surface. All he could see was me and all I could see was him. We were connected: I was on my knees, motionless, and he was stretching, pulling, extending, darting, and hurling sheets of sand to the wind.

It all happened so quickly, yet an eternity passed before me until once again we were nose to nose. I wasn't aware of Harold racing up, or David, or Max, or the others. They all knew something special had happened, and not only had they witnessed it, they had it on film. And I was pleased, too, demonstrating the power of love.

"That was fantastic," Harold exclaimed, startling me. I looked up, using my hand to shield my eyes from the sun.

"That was super. Unbelievable. I still don't believe it." Harold gasped for breath, hesitated, looked down at his camera, at Cougar, then back at his camera. "Do you think he could do that again?"

And he did, three times in all, not because he was hungry and racing for food, but because he wanted to be close to me. Then, after three runs, he gently tugged me back to the car. He wanted to go home and I understood.

5

CRYING WOLF—INSTINCT OR NOT

MOST OF OUR behavior is learned, meaning that we go through an experience, learn, remember, and react accordingly—right or wrong. Instincts, though, are just as powerful, but unlike learning, without any explanation as to why. They are illusive. We don't know why we're acting violent or compassionate—other than that it's just the way it is. These inherited feelings and actions are strings controlling us—out of sight, out of consciousness, but always there. We are born with them and we can never shake their influence.

All animals have instincts, whether a one-celled amoeba dividing or a young couple sunning on the beach one spring afternoon. People profess to be above instinctual behavior, asserting it's beneath them, but we are all animals. We may be technically more intelligent, but down deep, all animals are amazingly close, particularly with regard to instincts. The closer I got to Cougar, the more I understood that, instinctually, we were practically the same. Maybe I could temper my feelings better than he, but similar strings were tugging both of us in the same direction.

One instinct has to do with the importance of size. Most animals huff and puff to ward off an adversary; many can even make themselves look bigger. They didn't learn to do so, it just happens: they are programmed. It's because of size that dogs usually demand a higher place in the pecking order than cats, for they are normally larger and more domineering—that alpha instinct. But what about dogs' big brother, the wolf? Is he dominant to his cat neighbor, the mountain lion? Who is superior out in nature? For the wolf, it's not just a matter of an individual's size, because wolves travel in packs, making their combined strength significant, even to man. So we might proclaim the wolf sovereign. But not so fast.

Tales and folklore about mountain lions and wolves are mesmerizing. Exaggerations first arose back when one pioneer attempted to outdo another in talking about what he saw, how close he got, and so on. One such bit of lore is that mountain lions instinctively fear two creatures: man and the dog. Now, the idea of instinctively fearing something specific is depressing to me, like being committed to anxiety and consternation for no logical or apparent reason. At any rate, "experts" say that in the early history of the species, mountain lions were threatened by wolves, the canine ancestors of dogs, and somehow passed this fear along genetically. One argument against this notion, however, is that even though wolves aren't native to the southern hemisphere, the southern mountain lion, called a puma, is terrified of dogs. Yet its ancestors didn't encounter wolves. So this fear of dogs isn't because of wolves. But why does it exist? And what about this supposed fear of man? Leading authorities on the behavior of wolves theorize that mountain lions fear dogs because first they feared wolves, then dogs, then man with dogs. This all sounds like trying to make complicated sense out of something very simple.

Cougar fears neither man nor dog, eliminating two of the

three hypotheses from the start. I believed I knew the answer, but I had to introduce Cougar to a wolf pack to prove it. So one Saturday morning Linda, Cougar, and I hopped into the Jeep to visit Dr. Eric Klinghammer, the recognized leader in wolf behavior studies at his research facility. His fifty or so acres were just outside a one-horse town and could be reached by crossing a railroad track, turning left at a wood-floored country store, and traveling down a gravel road.

The entry gate was a dilapidated four-foot chain-link arrangement, probably donated for tax purposes after the original owner was going to throw it away anyway. And the guardhouse, which wouldn't protect anyone from the sun, much less the rain, leaned to the left under an elm tree, reminding me of a fort the local kids might have built.

As we approached, the gate was open and the guardhouse was vacant, so I idled by. I would have liked to take my pulse. I felt comfortable, but not as if I were arriving home. Could there be an autonomic, instinctual discomfort when entering someone else's territory? A small brick house was set back from the driveway to the left, and to the right was a filthy old barn with a muddy paddock surrounded by a split-rail fence. As I drove to the parking area, several roosters were pecking the dry ground.

Just beyond this dusty lot was a dilapidated bleacher with half-rotted planks flanking a tall chain-link enclosure for the wolves. Standing precariously on stilts in the corner was a ten-by-ten-foot observation tower that looked as if it belonged on the set of *Hogan's Heroes*. A dirt path snaked past the enclosure to a line of cages, some occupied, some not, stacked under a tin roof. Farther up the trail and almost out of sight was a little schoolhouse for meetings and lectures; a red fox was crammed into a small enclosure out front. And farther up the path and over the hill, I would later discover, were a dozen or so roaming bison for demonstrations of how wolves hunt.

As we pulled up and stopped, the dozen or so wolves were interacting, as two people in the tower—one with binoculars, the other taking notes—observed them. Two of the wolves casually glanced in our direction, then looked away, probably assuming, as people do, that the shadow in the back of my car was a dog. I'm sure they had seen visitors many times before and couldn't have cared less. But for Cougar this was brand-new. He was riveted to the window. Leaving Linda behind with Cougar, I went to check in at the observation tower.

"Hello," I said after climbing the rickety stairs. "There was no one at the gate, so I drove through. Hope that's okay."

"No problem," a young man of college age said, returning my smile. He was slight in build, still had a baby face, was dressed in jeans and a torn cotton shirt, and probably attended the college nearby. He had long, dark, curly hair, wore thick glasses, and had a trait of rarely making eye-to-eye contact— glancing down instead. Must have learned that from the wolves, I thought. Or was it instinct for him to glance down when someone entered his territory? He obviously wasn't the alpha male.

His associate was, at first, standoffish, as if I had interrupted her work. She looked directly into my eyes. She had long blondish-brown hair pulled into a ponytail and wore a drably colored oversized jacket and baggy jeans, neither of which hid the fact that she was forty or so pounds overweight for her five-foot-five frame. She took on a protective posture—had all the alpha qualities. I'll bet she acted the same when she was a little girl—was born that way.

"My name is Tod," the young man said, extending his hand and still glancing down. His grip reminded me of holding an injured pup. His nails were packed with grime. "And this is Patsy," he added.

"Hi, Patsy. Nice meeting you, Tod. I'm David. Anything interesting happening?" I said, displaying sincere interest, but also thinking that whatever the answer was, it wasn't going to compare with what was out in the car.

"Nah, pretty much same-o, same-o. Are you wolf people?"

"No, cat, though I love my golden," I said, beaming.

"At least your golden is descended from wolves," Patsy said, smiling for the first time.

"True," I answered, happy to get a response from her as I looked down at the wolves.

Tod and Patsy, in a human way, were acting just like Cougar. Cougar will hit the dirt and try to get invisible when someone approaches us on our walks. But after he listens and recognizes that they are not a threat, he begins to warm up. First his chin will come off the ground, then his ears will stand up, then his posture will relax, and then, finally, he'll look away.

In movies and nature films, wolves always appear clean and shiny. The wolves here were filthy. Most were biting at fleas and several had hairless spots with scabby sores.

"Who gives them baths?" I inquired, thinking they all desperately needed a flea bath, with attention paid to their ulcerations.

"We take turns hosing them down once a week, but they'll

just roll in the dirt," Patsy said with a laugh. "They're not pampered and live just like in the wild."

I didn't recall that rusty barbed wire was part of the wilderness scene. Neither was limiting the wolves' available space to the size of a small house. I don't remember seeing an observation tower and bleachers in the "wild," either. And I never saw a wildlife film on television showing mangy and seemingly underfed wolves. Maybe, in the wild, wolves would finish eating, swim in a mountain stream, and sun themselves dry on a carpet of grass. But I knew that seldom if ever happens. Funny how the wild is anything we want it to be, where most people believe the wildlife they displace will easily find its place elsewhere and live happily ever after. I continued observing what my eyes called neglect.

Finally I broke the silence. "I'm studying another predator sharing the top of the food chain with the wolf."

"Wolves aren't good at sharing," Tod said with a laugh.

"Funny, that's exactly why we're here. I'm trying to discover who is dominant, the mountain lion or the wolf."

"That's easy," Patsy declared, puffing with pride. "The wolf."

"That's what everyone seems to believe, but I'm not so sure," I answered with a sense of confidence.

"Interesting, but impossible to decide, unless you've got a mountain lion in your car," Tod kidded.

"As a matter of fact, I do," wondering if they had seen Cougar on an evening news segment aired a week before.

". . . on television the other night?" Patsy and Tod exclaimed in unison.

"Yep," I confessed.

"I'll be darned. We were all having dinner, commenting on

your story. Small world," Tod said with amazement. "Patsy, get the doctor."

As Patsy was leaving, Tod asked, "Does he really live in your home without a cage?"

"Yes. My philosophy is that you have to get close to understand—essentially live with to know. Once you understand, then you can help. This works with people, too."

Tod was persuaded, yet puzzled. "But with a wild animal?"

"Says who? People call animals wild because it's easy; doing so is a label from a hypocritical accuser. There is nothing that wolves or mountain lions do that is unique to them. Animals are animals, humans included. And when we don't understand an action, rather than trying to find out the reason, we toss it in the closet, shut the door, and label it wild, perpetuating our self-proclaimed sovereignty. Maybe we're afraid of the truth and really don't want to know that we act the same. And sometimes we're just wrong. For example, Cougar being instinctively afraid of wolves would be like you being born fearing zebras or something. I believe specifically learned fears shouldn't be confused with the general instinctive fears, like abrupt loud noises, and maybe the sense of falling."

"Interesting. Here comes the doctor."

A tall, slender, gray-haired man in his early sixties strode toward us with an authoritative gait. He too was dressed in a cross between safari and slum—the uniform of the day. He shook my hand vigorously but gave me a questioning glance.

"Saw you on television the other night. Hope your viewers didn't think they should do the same."

"I hope so, too," I answered. "And how about those who

come here to see your wolves?" This surprised the doctor. I'm sure he never considered that bringing people here might entice some to also get a wolf.

"But at least there is a lot more room here than in a house."

Granted, I thought, but space doesn't override neglect. Not wishing to get into an argument, I changed the subject: "I want to discover if mountain lions instinctively fear wolves. What's your opinion, Doctor."

"I believe they do."

"With your permission, I'd like to prove you wrong."

"Okay. Patsy, I'll be in the house. Let me know when the experiment begins. This is exciting."

And with an air of enthusiasm the doctor departed, as abruptly as if he had left something burning on the stove.

Tod and Patsy continued to educate me on wolf behavior as I observed how these wolves were different from mountain lions—basically in their physical closeness. What causes physical closeness or solitude? There must be a reason. I think with predators it's linked to the importance of capturing food.

"Alpha . . . leader . . . social . . . what do you think?" Patsy was asking me a question.

"Though the alpha male has privileges, I'm sure his responsibilities are tough," I said, putting several of her words together and guessing at her question.

Tod broke in, waving his hand, "Enough. I want to meet Cougar."

"All right," I said, smiling.

As we approached the car, Linda got out and I made the introductions.

After greeting Linda, Tod peered into our Grand Cherokee with tinted windows and watched Cougar watching the wolves.

"Is he frightened?" Tod asked.

"Not when his nose is writing 'wolf' on the window," I answered. I lowered the back window halfway, allowing both Tod and Patsy to extend the back of their hands. For once, Tod wasn't glancing down.

"Gosh, he's big. I had no idea . . . a lot larger than a wolf," he remarked. "Can you get him out?"

"I'll be glad to, but what about the doctor—?"

"It's all right," Patsy interrupted, shrugging her shoulders.

"But—"

"No, really, it'll be okay," Patsy insisted.

"Okay, the three of you stand over there, so as not to draw attention to Cougar."

I looked over at the house, hoping to see the doctor. Patsy must know what she's doing, I thought, as I opened the back door, snuggled cheek to cheek with Cougar, then attached his leash.

There were several vehicles parked to our left between Cougar and the wolves, but then there was nothing but thirty feet of dusty open space. Cougar didn't want to remain in the security of the car. He stepped down and out with resolve, looked toward the enclosure, then with confidence and determination slunk, half-stalk, half-walk, keeping the parked vehicles between himself and the wolves, and eventually peered around the fender of the last car in line.

The wolves were totally unaware of Cougar, which was surprising. Even if they couldn't see him, surely they would at least get a whiff of what was going on. But as I scanned the entire pack, none had the slightest clue that a mountain lion was there. The alpha male weighed approximately 120 pounds and there were two or three other males close to his size, though most members of the pack were smaller.

Cougar was two years old at the time and weighed just under 200 pounds. His body wasn't barrel-shaped like the wolves', but was flat like a sail, slipstreamed for speed. Straight on, if his head was low, one would just see a face crowned with rocking shoulders, but from the side his size became much more impressive.

For predators, size is an ace. Granted, there is security in numbers and the pack is important, but I believe it is only secondary to an individual's size. Cougar knew he was twice as big as most of the wolves and, importantly, they didn't see him. A cat inherently relies on stealth, whereas canines depend on numbers and instinctively communicate with the group. Dogs bark at an intruder; Cougar just hides. There is no one to call. Besides, making a noise forfeits the element of surprise. When you see a cat, it's too late. Now, in Mother Nature's game, Cougar held two aces, size and surprise, and the wolves held one, the pack. Cougar wasn't worried, for by nature's rules, a pair of aces beats one of a kind.

There was nothing but open space between Cougar and the wolves. He would have to step out into the open, but he could press them, converting surprise into fear. If he elected to turn and run, the wolves would want to chase him. If the wolves were across a field, given their numbers and without the advantage of surprise, Cougar would be in trouble. But this was different; he stepped from around the car and walked, head low, pupils dilated, whiskers stabbing toward the wolves, ears slanted forward, shoulders rocking, each paw creating a mushroom of dust as it struck the ground.

His image caused absolute havoc. The pack was threatened and looked to the alpha male for protection. But "Alpha" was, at best, reluctant—I'd call him scared. His eyes were riveted on Cougar. He looked down, licked his lips, whimpered, and turned sideways. Immediately one of the larger males snipped at Alpha's hindquarters, provoking a skirmish, which quickly ended with both males staring at Cougar. Another confrontation broke out between two other males, and another, and another.

The doctor flew out of the house, ran toward the enclosure, and skidded to a halt. His face was crimson, his jaw grated, his fists trembled (all instinctive responses). The entire pack was in disarray, but that wasn't why he was mad. Cougar strolled over to a grassy area under a tree approximately eight feet from the chain-link fence, lay down, and began licking his paws, watching the disjointed wolves. The doctor screamed, "Patsy, why didn't you get me? How many chances will I have to experience a mountain lion confronting the wolves? You are so selfish . . . selfish . . . selfish."

After this outburst, all was quiet except for the wolves. The doctor first glanced at Cougar—who, if he had been any more comfortable, would have been napping—then at the wolves. Their powerful epoxy-like social structure was shredded. The doctor looked dejected, as if his favored team had lost and, keeping his gaze to the ground, he said, "I think you should take Cougar away from the wolves."

"Join us, please," I insisted.

"Yes, I'd like that. Maybe I could observe how other animals react to Cougar," he said, casting a stare at Patsy that, if it had been teeth, would have had her by the throat. Patsy looked away and down. It was obvious who was the alpha.

"Let's take a walk," I said to Cougar, who immediately sprang to his feet and walked away from the enclosure, toward a dairy farm across the way. From Cougar's perspective it was time to go. Cats want as much of an advantage as possible—a survival thing. Once the surprise was over, it was down to size and numbers. The wolves were behind a fence, so it didn't matter, but the odds now favored them and it was time to go. Linda remained behind with the Jeep.

"And he's voice-trained too," the doctor commented, ramming his hands into his pockets, his face starting to regain its natural color.

"Not as well as dogs," I said, "and mainly when he wants to."

"Kind of like me," the doctor said with a chuckle. Then, with the beginning of a smile, he spoke again. "I actually began my studies with large cats, but because of unrelated circumstances at the time, I turned to studying wolves. Wonder how the cows will react to Cougar."

A barbed-wire fence was strung along a natural barrier of elm and maple trees. Tall weeds and vines encircled the rusty wire as if Mother Nature objected to the intrusion. On the other side was a herd of cows grazing, and farther in the distance were bright white buildings of the dairy.

"Will they stampede?" the doctor asked.

"I doubt it. Not unless Cougar runs toward them. My guess is that they'll just chew and watch."

As our threesome approached, every cow eye was on Cougar. And when Cougar is among people, the same thing happens. It's the predator's fate.

Getting the undivided attention of a field of cows was strange. They'd gawk, bend down, grab a quick clump of grass, raise up, and chew. Maybe a hundred cows, eyes riveted and mouths moving in unison—Cougar's answer to the "Got milk?" commercial.

"I wonder what the bison would do," the doctor said, getting into the science of it.

"My guess, the same as the cows, but you're the bison expert."

"Let's find out."

We began to trek toward the bison field. The doctor looked at the ground as he walked and, after several seconds of silence, asked, "Why wasn't Cougar afraid of the wolves?"

I smiled. "One, two, three. First, I believe general fears can be instinctive, but not specific ones like fearing certain animals. Second, relative size is extremely important. And third is the manner of a closing motion."

The doctor looked puzzled. "Manner?"

I continued: "Over the eons it has been the temperament of prey to run and of predators to chase; it's their being, their instinct. When hunting dogs chase a top-of-the-food-chain mountain lion, it's all wrong for the cat. It's not the way he's instinctively set up. He's scared. If it were possible to change the temperament of a deer and have him run toward a mountain lion, I truly believe the lion would feel threatened and run away. As for the wolves, they weren't moving. Cougar recognized that he was larger, relied on the element of surprise, and closed on them. But reverse everything, have the wolves rush Cougar, and he would have felt threatened."

The doctor nodded, saying under his breath, "So lions don't fear dogs, just the manner in which the dogs pursue them."

"Yes. Closure distinguishes predator from prey. It's the predator's surprise that initiates the prey's flight, and the closure is on. Even when a predator rushes another predator, the one that is rushing holds the cards and, even if smaller, can bluff until the fleeing predator turns to fight. But that doesn't normally happen. Even we become uncomfortable when someone rushes us. It's the same thing. And what is the first thing people do when encountering a mountain lion in the woods? They turn and run, which isn't a good idea, for they may be triggering a prey instinct from the lion to chase us down."

"Hmm."

We continued walking.

"Let's walk this way; it's shorter," the doctor said, pointing to the left.

"Not for Cougar," I answered. "Instinctively, he walks along or next to something. We will make much better time by continuing to walk along this fence line, rather than out in the open. Cougar will choose to track the two sides of a right triangle, walking next to something before traversing the hypotenuse out in the open. The reason many people believe he is so well leash-trained is that I know where he wants to go. He's on rails; I could do this without his leash."

The doctor laughed. He thought about the idea of unleashing Cougar for a moment, then abandoned it. "What if you want to take him across an open field?"

"It'd be easy to guide Cougar anywhere I want. I just know what makes him the most comfortable."

After ten more minutes of walking, the doctor looked up toward the field of bison and yelled: "Here, bison, bison, bison! Here, bison, bison, bison!"

Maybe one shaggy ox looked in our direction.

"Here, bison, bison!"

No response. The entire herd of bison couldn't have cared less. Granted, they were fifty yards away . . . but nothing? No reaction?

"I know they are alive," I said, laughing. "Their tails are moving. Maybe they're living in the past."

"There's more to that than you might think," said the doctor. "Here, bison, bison, bison!"

Still nothing.

"Where do you normally do your shows?" I asked.

"Over there," the doctor said, pointing.

"Do you think they don't react to you because you're not in the right place, in essence, don't recognize you?"

He yelled out again, "Here, bison, bison!" and added, "They always react to my call."

"Okay, while they're making up their minds, there's a question I've wanted to ask you."

"Shoot."

"I've found that the dilation of the pupils is very indicative. For example, a cat with dilated pupils can be dangerous. How do you read a wolf?"

The doctor paused for a moment, then spoke. "If you are close enough to see their pupils, you're too close."

"That's your answer?" I said, disappointed.

"That's it."

How sad, I thought. "Should we be heading back?" I inquired.

"Sure," the doctor answered, inhaling deeply, taking in all the openness, giving me a chance to deliberate on instincts.

AN INSTINCT IS an inborn tendency to behave in a way characteristic of a species. My question is: How specific do we get? Cats, dogs, people, like all other mammals, share the suckling instinct, and I believe it goes much further than that. So which instincts do we share, let's say with cats, and which ones are different? It's difficult to compare, us to them, because their instincts seem closer to the surface. My explanation is that their lives, both past and present, haven't changed that much. Man, on the other hand, has been advancing so quickly technologically that many of his natural instincts are no longer critical to his survival. Over the years they have been pushed farther and farther back into the recesses of his mind—but they're still there. For humans, the suckling instinct has remained strong because that behavior still remains important to our survival. But it's impossible for any potential new instincts to keep up with our constantly changing environment; anything important today will be outdated tomorrow. So, in essence, technology is both over-riding and suppressing instincts. That will work just fine until we're stripped of our science, as in having to temporarily fend for ourselves out in the wilderness or, God forbid, a world catastrophe. In those types of circumstances, because of our weakened survival instincts, we are doomed, unlike a pampered house cat who could be abandoned in the woods and survive.

But could Cougar instinctively fear something specific, because of the possibility that it remains as appropriate today as it was for his ancestors, even though wolves are not a threat of this kind? Could cats, specifically Cougar, instinctively fear another animal?

And what about the opposite of fear: security? There can be no argument that Cougar seeks out corners and prefers being against something. So if he instinctively feels security, can instinctive fears be so different? I believe the key to all this, again, is, How specific do we get? Security and fear are general emotions, whereas reaction to a particular animal is very precise and is learned.

Cougar is very uncomfortable around snakes. He watches intently as they slither through the grass, but he'll never approach. And if I catch one, he backs up and hisses. This fear was learned in seconds when Cougar was only six months old and walking with me in an Indianapolis park. I was frightened when he approached a rattlesnake and shouted that he back up. He's been apprehensive of snakes ever since. And he's deathly afraid of horses ever since a man on horseback rushed us as we took an evening walk. These specific fears are learned.

What's not to love?

Sleepy time.

Cougar
playing
with
Chivas.

How do birds
do this?

The
devil made
me chew
the couch.

Top: So how does the other half live?

Right: Cougar pulling anchor.

Bottom: Cougar chasing Dad in the park.

Opposite page top: Me teaching Cougar the backstroke.

Opposite page bottom: Cougar keeping an eye on feathered friends.

Top: Six-year-old Cougar meeting his birthday present.

Left: So what do you do in a situation like this? Read on.

Cougar just stepped on a burr and is about to lick it away.

A great demonstration of phlegming.

"LET'S WALK TO the schoolhouse. I think you'll find it interesting," the doctor said, pointing forty-five degrees to the right.

"Yes, that will be fine," I answered, knowing the walk would allow me time to continue reflecting.

I RECALLED THE day, in early spring, when Cougar and I were hiking on mushy ground in an Indianapolis park off Fall Creek Boulevard. I'd watch him stop, shake his paws, then continue plopping them into the dampness. A musky scent saturated the air and the sun beat down, loosening winter's defiant grasp. Cougar walked beside me—unless an unsuspecting squirrel was on the ground far from a tree. Guided by instinct, he'd rocket away, only to rejoin me seconds later, chirping to explain how close he had come. His reaction to animals differs depending on their size, distance, and movement. He reacts instantly to a small animal darting close by and is always methodical and calculative with distant deer. For raccoons and other midsize animals, his reaction is somewhere in the middle. He didn't learn any of these reactions, but was genetically coded as a feline predator—a code into which man, standing erect, doesn't fit.

On that particular walk, the ground concealed the sound of my passage, since nothing was dry enough to snap, but for Cougar it was the same old silence, with just an occasional slurping noise as his paw broke suction with the muck. Then suddenly he froze, indicating the presence of a large animal in the distance. Yes, there she was, a doe, approximately sixty yards away, nibbling on nature's afternoon offerings. Her size revealed that this spring was not something new to her. But what had her in his sight was. She had never experienced a worthy predator and therefore kept eating. Every time she lowered her head to grab a mouthful of grass, Cougar would scoot ahead, straight as an arrow, on his stomach, as if he were weightlessly skipping along with shoulder blades rocking and hips rolling. His legs were at every angle but straight, conjuring up an image of a supersonic katydid. Every time the doe looked up, he froze. Finally she became suspicious, perhaps wondering why this tan blob was so much closer, yet had never moved. Cougar was following a stalking procedure that had worked well for millions of years; he was programmed.

The doe stood motionless, focused on Cougar for what seemed an eternity, then began to chew again without relinquishing her stare. Cougar didn't blink. Then she guardedly lowered her head. If I myself realized that Cougar had but one more chance to close the distance, I'm sure it was obvious to him. As the doe was nibbling grass he took off again, sucked to the ground like a Wave Runner in smooth waters until that magical moment: from sliding fifteen miles per hour on his stomach, he now started running, instantly accelerating to full stride, jackhammering the surface, leaving murky craters and spray in his wake.

The doe exploded into action. She zigzagged, and every time she did, Cougar ratcheted closer. When she vaulted fifteen feet, Cougar hurdled ten. He was reducing the distance traveled both horizontally and vertically and seemed to anticipate her every move, as if she had turn signals.

Cougar was faster, but he also closed in by running a shorter distance. I'm sure it is nature's plan for highly maneuverable prey to outmaneuver their predators by jackrabbitting away, but Cougar seemed to know her every move. And the winter hadn't weakened him; he was strong, rested, and well fed. He would continue the chase until his muscles were on fire, and after seventy-five yards (a marathon by lion standards) I'm sure they were. Cougar closed in as the doe darted along the river. I thought success was his until she leapt off an eight-foot cliff into the frigid water. And before I knew it, Cougar was airborne, too. Her vault was thirty feet. She hit the water like a cannonball and Cougar splashed in ten feet behind her with a muffled sound; he was stealthy even when diving into the water.

The doe, swept along by the fierce current and with Cougar in her wake, set her sights on the opposite bank. Cougar's paws are webbed like paddles compared to the doe's sticklike hooves, so he continued closing. To my horror, though, the other side of the river was a restricted military base. *I* was restricted from going there, much less Cougar. Now, I never want to let Cougar out of my sight. When I do leave him at home alone, he is inside and protected. Even if he were outside in an enclosure (which is never), I'd want to oversee him—there are just too many things that could go wrong.

To keep Cougar in sight I had but one choice: jump into a thirty-two-degree river with a current mighty enough to transport fallen trees. And if I did make it to the other side, I'd be on the grounds of a restricted military base without permission— not good.

"Cougar!" I screamed at the top of my lungs. Then again, my voice detonating with desperation, "Cooougaarrr!"

I don't know if my voice quavered because of the shouting, the emotion, or both, but after my second shrieking appeal, he spun around. I felt like a shaken bottle of champagne. I was filled with the exuberance of getting Cougar to turn around in the middle of a chase.

I dropped to my knees, scooted backwards, and lowered myself over the edge of the cliff, inching down, landing on broken-up concrete slabs dumped there to curb erosion. Cougar looked as if he had just lost fifty pounds as he dragged his drenched body up from the river. I threw my arms around him. After I told him how great he was for answering my calls, I glanced back at the eight-foot cliff scooped away at the bottom by the flooded river the day before. There was nothing to grab hold of, or step up on, to help me scale the sandy wall.

"Okay, your instinct got us into this problem; now your learning will get us out," I told Cougar in a low, deliberate tone, attaching his leash and pointing to the top of the cliff. "You go first. Come on." And at my last command, Cougar leapt to the top of the cliff. For a moment all I could see was sky. Had he taken off? Then, there he was, sheepishly peering over the ledge, with the other end of the leash in his mouth.

"That's it, drop it," I requested. He just stood motionless; then, after another command, he dropped the end of the leash. I don't know if I was more thrilled at being rescued or at how it was done. I grabbed the black nylon leash dangling in front of me and began inching up the cliff, being careful not to tug too hard, using the leash primarily to remain upright, so that I could kick my feet into the sand. After inching up, I peered over the top and was nose to nose with my savior. His collar was pulled up over his ears and his chin and front paws were braced in the sand, like an unwilling dog being pulled by his owner. I rocked back and forth, worming myself up the rest of the way, trying to lessen the force on Cougar's collar.

They'll never believe this, I thought, adjusting his collar back down around his neck and petting him vigorously as he gave me a look saying that I really must get hold of my emotions.

THE DOCTOR'S VOICE recalled me to the present. "And this is the schoolhouse, but I call it my lecture hall," he said, beaming with pride as he opened the door.

Just then, Linda drove up with the Jeep. Great timing, I thought. I asked the doctor to excuse me for a moment, saying that I was going to put Cougar back in the car because he was probably thirsty. Cougar walked as if on rails to the back door of the car.

"That was perfect timing," I said to Linda.

Linda beamed back. "I saw you walking this way and stopping at the school, so I thought Cougar would be more comfortable in here."

"Yep, perfect," I said again, unfastening his lead and closing the door. I watched as he went right for his water bowl piled high with ice and started lapping away, rattling the ice cubes against the side.

The doctor had gone inside, giving me more time to think as I slowly walked back toward the school.

I THOUGHT ABOUT another example of Cougar's instinctual behavior, this time with both a groundhog and a deer in Dayton,

Ohio, a city that has what are called metro parks—expansive wild-life areas close to offices, motels, and restaurants. A metro park is really a perfect place to take a leisurely walk or have lunch.

Cougar and I were enjoying a perfect autumn afternoon, when the temperature makes you forget that winter is just around the corner and the sun illuminates seemingly electric trees. Cougar was anxious to get out of the car as we pulled up and stopped at a remote clearing. Several picnic tables were scattered about and the entire area was surrounded by forest. There was a car parked next to us and in it was a man having a sandwich with the windows rolled down, presumably enjoying an hour of relaxation before going back to work. A distant groundhog fed on grass at the forest's edge, unaware that he himself might be lunch.

I got out and walked over to the parked car.

"Hello," I said.

"Yes, hi," the man responded, putting his book on his lap. He was maybe in his late fifties, with receding gray hair and wire-rimmed glasses like my grandfather used to wear.

"I don't wish to disturb you, but I wanted to ask if it'd be all right to let my cat out for a walk," I inquired with a smile.

"Of course," he answered, almost laughing.

"Oh, one more thing," I said. "He weighs two hundred pounds."

The man's head snapped to the right. He peered at the outline barely visible through my tinted windows smeared with nose prints—smudges that didn't obstruct Cougar's view.

"I thought you had a dog. Sure, I'd love it."

"Okay, I will be letting him out of the car without a leash

and he will try to catch that groundhog over there. After that, I'll put his leash on and we'll walk into the woods."

"Just like that," the man said in amazement. "May I get out?"

"Sure, just don't run," I answered, with a laugh.

I opened the back door of the Suburban. A hunting situation is the only one in which I have to loop my finger around Cougar's collar after opening the door, for he wants to get on with the hunt. I grabbed his leash, wrapped it around my neck like a bolo tie, scanned the area for anything moving, nodded to our excited spectator, and announced, "Okay," to Cougar.

He slunk from the car, stopping with his front paws on the ground and his rear still up in the car, looking around the door toward the groundhog. This would be impossible for him. There was nothing to camouflage his advance. Just a thirty-yard carpet of unobstructed grass, with a picnic table off line.

But it was fun to try, time for the supersonic katydid and the limbo performed upside down, as I followed close behind. Groundhogs are seldom far from their burrow. This big fella, large enough to threaten any self-respecting house cat, just munched away as Cougar scooted and froze, scooted and froze, unbelievably to just ten feet away. Then there was a loud squeak as the groundhog realized something was up and scurried the short distance to his burrow. Cougar leapt and landed just where the oversize rodent had disappeared. I, of course, didn't instruct Cougar on any of this behavior. It was locked away in his genes, as with all cats. The only difference is size.

"Good boy," I shouted, clapping as I ran. Cougar chirped, walking toward me, waiting for my usual complimentary hugs. This is the time I mustn't dally. Cougar's focus on the hunt was gone and I needed to leash him before something else popped up. "You're such a good boy!" I cheered, scratching under his chin and stroking his body as he purred almost loud enough for the man leaning on his car to hear. "Such a good boy, you almost caught that groundhog!" I attached his lead, stood up, returned the man's wave and walked into the woods.

Above us to the right was a trail big enough for a car. And it wasn't long before a ranger's truck idled by. The truck was olive green with yellow lettering, but everything else was obstructed by brush and trees. Unless one was extremely observant, Cougar would appear to be a large dog. But this ranger was different. It wasn't long before she was walking up the path.

"Hello."

"Hi," I answered.

"I saw what you were walking, or should I say what was walking you, and just had to get a closer look." A woman in her thirties, wearing olive pants and a matching shirt, hesitated fifteen feet before me. She had stopped at a distance that, when approaching Cougar, should be traversed only after he feels comfortable. And it didn't take an expert to know that the time wasn't now. Cougar's head and body were down on the ground, like the stripe on a highway, and his ears were flat, horizontal, pointing to the sides like wings. From his perspective, we were all alone when, out of nowhere, someone approached, and he wanted to be invisible—blend in with the pebbles on the path—until deciding it was okay. This is all instinctive; he's never been attacked. He's insecure out in the open.

As we talked, Cougar recognized by my body actions that this lady wasn't threatening. First his ears came up, then he started looking around. He has learned all my signals demonstrating that everything is okay—if I'm okay, he's okay.

"My name is Pat. May I join you?" she asked.

Pat was delightful company, though I would have preferred to walk alone. It's work walking with Cougar when anyone is around—someone else to consider. But I really couldn't decline since we were, after all, walking in her park and not in the normal manner. Consideration is all-important when doing something different. I love those signs stating that dogs must be leashed, or are prohibited beyond a certain point. So what about cats? Doing something different, we frequently slip between the cracks and the secret is not taking advantage, but being considerate in a nonconforming sort of way.

"Sure. I'm David," I answered. "Just walk at a forty-five-degree angle behind us."

"Interesting. Why?"

"Follow behind him and he is protective, but walk in front and he is focused. If you cross that line, his whiskers will flick forward. And when that happens, you know you are under suspicion. All these are instinctive behaviors; I didn't teach him any of it."

"Gosh, this is fantastic . . . walking with a mountain lion. I wish some of his cousins lived here. The deer have decimated this park."

"You've got one today."

"Yeah, but he's on a leash."

"He doesn't have to be."

"Won't he run away?"

"No."

"You mean we just walk along until he sees a deer and then you let him go?"

"And I'll try to keep him in sight, but he'll return."

Just then, Cougar froze.

"There are three deer over there," I whispered, pointing straight ahead.

They were grazing in a field dense with small trees, but Cougar wasn't looking directly at them.

"Over here," I pointed out to Cougar, taking his head and twisting it fifteen degrees to the right. But he just returned his stare to the left.

"I can't believe he's missing them," I said, almost embarrassed.

Then, only fifteen yards away, I saw what Cougar was staring at: a smaller deer, looking directly at us. I whispered to Pat: "Shall we?"

"Absolutely!"

I unfastened Cougar's leash. He took several slow cautious steps into the brush and dropped to the ground. His tail began thrashing and his hips rocked back and forth in excitement.

The supersonic katydid wasn't necessary, for the deer was close, close enough to catch without stalking, which is amazing to me, because though Cougar wasn't experienced at chasing deer, he instinctively knew when he could catch them. After several seconds of remaining in place, shoulders rocking and hips rolling (maybe nature's way of warming up the joints), Cougar exploded forward. The earth once blanketed with autumn leaves was cratered by this force and the deer didn't wait to discover the cause. The cause was on.

Both prey and predator zigzagged away in the direction of my car as I attempted to keep up. I thought about the gentleman reading and imagined both Cougar and deer racing into view. Telling the groundhog story would be unbelievable enough. Now what about this? I can allow Cougar to enjoy these things without the possibility of his harming any park visitors because focus allows even more control than a leash. When Cougar is focused, nothing else is important to him, so human bystanders are perfectly safe. Predators don't bluff by looking one way and moving another. There is no chance of his physically harming anyone. My task goes beyond that: not to startle anyone, which a mountain lion running through the brush has a tendency to do. But finding space so Cougar can play without a human presence is practically impossible. People are everywhere.

Twenty yards in front of me the deer and Cougar raced behind dense foliage. I hate it when that happens. I like to keep my eyes on Cougar. When I circled the thicket, there he was. Cougar had stopped, waiting for me—an interruption from his instincts that was learned. He wanted to remain close. And, unbelievably, when he stopped, so did the deer.

After I caught up, Cougar was comfortable with me now close by and the chase continued. In a flash, he ran then leapt, knocking the deer to the ground, both of them rolling over and over. Cougar was like a spider, always on top, spinning a cocoon of dust and debris. And when they finally came to rest, Cougar's weight pinned the deer to the ground, both bodies gasping for air.

Stalking and chasing are instinctive. And once the prey is

caught, it is instinctive for Cougar to go for the back of the neck, unlike other species of cats, which go for the throat. Cougar never goes for the throat; he is programmed otherwise. For small animals, at this point it's normally all over but the memories, but mountain lions cannot kill deer without using what's called a killing bite. They must learn through experience—and some say must be taught by the mother—how to use their canine teeth surgically to penetrate between neck vertebrae of the deer. Of course Cougar has neither the experience nor the training from his mother, so at the very most he instinctively nibbles around the back of the deer's head and releases her—the "catch and release" policy.

ONCE MORE BACK to the present, I opened the door and walked into the schoolhouse, where the doctor was waiting to show me newspaper clippings about himself and his facility. There was a musty smell, as if we had gone back in time, and this again drove me back to my thought on instincts.

MOUNTAIN LIONS ARE suppose to be instinctively solitary, certainly not team players, but Cougar has learned to team up with me. One example among hundreds was when we were hiking on a summer day and a rabbit darted in front of us and dashed into a large area of tall grass beside the trail. Cougar just lowered his head and stared, making a guttural scoffing noise indicating that he was frustrated, since the possibility of catching something that fast, hidden by dense foliage, was remote. He always makes this sound of frustration after seeing an enticing animal he can't catch.

I think this reaction is quite revealing. Animal experts try to make sense out of predators not chasing possible prey that are too small by saying that they want to conserve energy—the energy it would take to chase and catch, compared to the energy provided by eating. This is a another complicated human explanation. Visualize a cat contemplating that a prey animal is too small and will louse up his conservation-of-energy plans. The fact of the matter is that cats are prudently lazy; the experts can call it anything they want. Dogs will run after something until they drop, but mountain lions quickly realize that small swift animals are exceedingly difficult to catch. Rabbits are so fast and can change direction so quickly that it takes an animal similar in size, like an eagle or a hawk, to outmaneuver them. Cougar may be fast, but changing direction as quickly as a rabbit is difficult for him. Deer are the perfect prey animal for mountain lions, not because lions are thinking about energy efficiency, but because the two animals are comparable in mass, accelerating, decelerating, and changing direction similarly. It's natures way, using simple physics, of ensuring that predators do in fact conserve energy and cats learn through experience which animals, by their relative size, are suitable prey.

But cats are opportunists, too. There is a record of a healthy and plump mountain lion who subsisted all summer long on grasshoppers because they were easy to catch, but as a rule predators size up their prey. Birds and squirrels out of reach up in a tree are not appealing to mountain lions. But have one of them compromised in some way and the opportunistic cat will give it a whirl.

Before leaving the subject of birds, I want to say there is a particular group that always gets Cougar's undivided attention: birds of prey. He will glue his gaze on a hawk or eagle swooping down or perched in a tree. And there once was a baby owl, smaller than my fist, grasping the side of a palm tree and Cougar attempted to scale that tree without claws. I wonder if it has to do with the fact that raptors, unlike any other bird but like all predators, have eyes in front of their heads. Or maybe they make a distinctive high-pitched sound that we cannot hear. Well, back to Cougar and me teaming up against a rabbit.

I pointed straight up with my index finger, indicating that Cougar should wait a moment. He was all eyes and ears. I then walked around the grassy area, circling around behind the rabbit. Cougar knew exactly what I was doing, so he crouched down, watched, and waited.

I entered the grass from the opposite end and began walking toward Cougar. His tail began thrashing back and forth. I was three-quarters of the way back, but still no rabbit. Maybe it had slipped away. I hoped not. I would lose credibility.

Then came that swish of a swift animal darting through dry grass as the rabbit sped away from me, directly toward our "little" surprise, then disappeared into his hole. You can't win them all. The same team tactic works with squirrels and groundhogs. Cougar and I will even split up and walk in opposite directions around a thicket. And since I make more noise than he, any unsuspecting animal will inevitably run from me, right to Cougar. Without teamwork rabbits are nearly impossible to catch.

Then there are opossums. No teamwork is necessary for

these seemingly prehistoric nocturnal rodents with the speed of a three-legged tortoise. During night walks Cougar will suddenly bolt into the darkness and stop. That's how long it takes to catch an opossum. And as he is mouthing the back of the opossum's neck, I hear crunching and popping noises until he drops a seemingly lifeless form to the ground. I'm sure it's dead.

We continue walking, then he always wants to return several minutes later to check out his prize, but the opossum is gone. Cougar has caught the same opossum three times; each time I was sure the poor creature was dead, but it just vanished into the night after playing possum.

"THEN THERE WAS this article about my studies on wolves," said the doctor, reeling me back to the present.

I recognized his associates in the picture, too. "How long have Tod and Patsy been with you?" I asked.

"Oh, about three years, I guess," he answered, inspecting the pictures of the past.

He was proud and I listened for fifteen or so minutes until an appropriate pause. "Shall we get back to Cougar? Linda has driven him back to the wolf enclosure," I said, watching the doctor savoring the past.

"She won't let him out, will she?" the doctor said with a snap.

"Oh, no, I'm the only one who walks Cougar," I answered. I felt good. I was proud that another person now knew the truth about mountain lions and wolves.

WALKING BACK WITH the doctor allowed my mind to wander again. The question still lingered: Can Cougar instinctively fear a particular animal? Not long ago I was walking Cougar through Florida swamplands one moonlit night. He was having the time of his life in the desolation. My fondness for places such as this has to do with the fact that Cougar likes them and people don't, giving us time to be alone. He seldom wanders more than twenty yards away. But if he does, I have learned not to worry, for he is playing a game. I'll continue hiking and out of nowhere he will spring, tag me on the leg, and scamper away. I'm it!

It was 1 A.M. and I'd had all the fun I could stand for one evening, with the mosquitoes, muck, and thorns. I reached over, attaching his leash to commence the fifteen-minute trek back to the car. The brush grabbed my light jacket like Velcro and at times was so dense I had to remove Cougar's leash and follow him on my hands and knees.

It looked as if I were taking part in a military survival training exercise—jeans soaked at the knees and socks and shoes covered with mud. But Cougar continued without a hair out of place, his sleek silhouette glistening. To him this voyage was effortless. My survival instincts were a little rusty.

The moon did little more than provide a reference point; its light was slashed to ribbons by the time it had filtered through the canopy of trees and brush. I normally didn't have this much amusement with him—thank God. This murky hell was webbed with streams that snaked through the marsh, eventually dumping their brackish water into the Gulf of Mexico. I wanted to ford just such a stream and indicated to Cougar where we should do it. But he would have none of it. I got behind him with my legs together and tried to scoot him into the water, but he just dug in.

Cougar *loves* the water. He'll jump out of a moving boat when the day is warm, but will insist on circumventing a puddle in the middle of the sidewalk—a cat thing. So I thought that I'd go first, to demonstrate that everything was all right. I wrapped the lead around my wrist and started to cross at a point twelve feet across and several feet deep. Wading deeper, I pleaded in a cutsie tone that he was being silly: "See, this water isn't going to bite you."

Then, suddenly, in a fraction of a second it became breathlessly clear why Cougar didn't care to cross. The moon's light, which a second before reflected a smooth and tranquil surface, now revealed violence: water being slashed and slapped from the center of the stream outward, side to side, by a ten-foot alligator. In the shadows, the entire stream undulated, up and down.

And since the end of Cougar's leash was looped tightly around my wrist, I had only one way to safety: back to him. But yanking on it would pull him into the water. It's funny, but in that split second when all seemed lost, I was concerned about his safety. And I believe his thoughts were about me as I made a frantic attempt, without pulling on his lead, to scoop the water with my hands to get back. I stared into his eyes with near-hopelessness. Then he crouched down and rocketed into the air, arching past me, brushing my face and landing on the other side. The lead wrenched my body around like a string whirling a top and I was yanked from the murky bottom, catapulted toward the opposite side, hitting just inches from the bank, and dragged into the brush, where I landed on my chin.

The water was silent. Cougar walked back to me and we bumped noses. Then he placed his face next to mine and held it there. I was shivering—the result of excitement and being soaked to the bone. Without a sound, I began brushing the wet sand from his back legs as a tear crept down my face. He licked it away.

Was Cougar instinctively frightened of alligators, or just apprehensive of something different? My thought: He was just uneasy, because mountain lions, past and present, don't normally come into contact with alligators, most certainly not a northern species like Cougar. But right then, with all my desire to know the answer, I really didn't care.

It was the doctor's proud voice that brought me back as we walked. Learning about animals can do that. I should know.

6

NEIGHBORS—NATURAL AND NOT

ONE OF MY major pleas is for people to knowledgeably become good neighbors with wildlife—nature's creatures living in harmony with our homes. We can learn the big-cat side from Cougar and the human side from my neighbors. After all, Cougar is a mountain lion with the same instincts as his wildlife brethren, and my neighbors most likely represent a reasonable cross-section of society. Some are, at first, ecstatic and some apprehensive about having Cougar as a neighbor. But in every case, apprehension, if any, has disappeared and appreciation soared. Cougar is even invited to neighborhood parties (which, of course, is not what I'm advocating). One reason is that when you pare away all the sensationalism, mountain lions protect the status quo. They don't wish things to change.

So what is it like to live next to a mountain lion? I believe this chapter demonstrates not only what people can learn from mountain lions, but what lions can learn from people. This in spite of the fact that Cougar is used to living with humans, which could be considered a disadvantage, since he is comfortable with people whereas his wildlife cousins want nothing more than to be left alone.

Cougar's first home with Linda and me was a spacious lakeside house on Tenacious Drive in Indianapolis, Indiana. But life took a nosedive—adversity. At least that's the way it looked at the time. In my case, it was diabetes upsetting the aviation applecart, leaving me only one sensible option: Deal with it.

What a change that was: Cougar, Chivas, Regal, Linda, and me, having to squeeze into a thirty-foot recreational vehicle, bringing up the proverbial question regarding changing conditions and pets. Would Fido or Fluffy be better off somewhere else? My answer is, probably not. We should be concerned not only with our pets' physical health, but with their mental well-being. Too many times, finding a new home for the cat or dog has little to do with their welfare. We rationalize to make ourselves feel better, saying Fido has got more room now or Fluffy has got someone to play with, when the simple truth of the matter often is that we don't want to be bothered. When we decide to get a pet, we should consider its life expectancy and what we plan on doing within that time frame. If family members are considered part of a lifelong alliance, then what makes animals any different? We are, after all, talking about a life.

But it's only natural for humans to feel superior to animals, however wrong it may be. Let's ask an extraterrestrial alien, who is obviously vastly more intelligent than we just by the fact that he can visit Earth, who it is that he considers superior—himself or us. The answer is obvious. Does that mean he has the right to displace us or even destroy us if he sees fit? It would be hypocritical to say that he didn't have that right, for we usually treat animals that way. "Do unto others" should apply to all life forms, not just to humans. Consequently it was my decision not to abandon Cougar, Chivas, or Regal, but to try to make the best of the situation.

WE WERE INVITED to hook up to electricity and water on a friend's farm, where we met Rodan the rooster, Gunter the Labrador, Toby the springer spaniel, and Puss-Ann the cat, along with Scotty and Failey, the two horses. Cool breezes, puffy clouds, gnarly trees, sweet clover, muddy barn, and a white farmhouse, all surrounded by oceans of corn, were our new home.

We were newcomers. Cougar, at one and a half years old, got respect because of who he was. Ten-year-old Chivas, on the other hand, with his glazed face, rested unintrusively in the shade of the front porch, content to be a bystander. Eventually he was welcome anywhere and everywhere—at the foot of the owner's bed, in front of the kitchen fan when afternoons were hot, in a shady area of grass where Rodan wanted to roost, on Toby's blanket, or drinking from Gunter's bowl. No one objected. By intimidating no one, Chivas wedged into everybody's heart. Then tragedy struck.

It was on the fifth of July. Chivas became ill when all medical facilities were either closed or didn't return our calls. Vomiting was the first sign that he wasn't well. Was it intestinal torsion, a toxin, or maybe the cumulative effect of ten years' living? Chivas's face was like a ghost's as he labored to breathe. We were all with him on the porch that night. Yes, he was weak, but I was confident he'd be making his daily rounds tomorrow.

Linda and I were the last to leave. I moistened his lips with water and whispered that he was my "bestest boy." He stretched his neck back, straining to see me leave. Early the next morning it was clear that he hadn't moved. One by one, all his animal friends honored him. Reverently they circled his body, keeping their distance, seemingly out of respect. They had opened their home and hearts to him. Now they had their fan, favorite places, blankets, and bowls back, but what they wanted was Chivas.

Cougar was different. He didn't have free rein of the property; I was supposed to restrict him to certain areas. But one day, rather than walking him around the directed side of the barn, I walked him around the farmhouse side, so as not to upset the chickens who congregated in our path. We then left for the weekend and upon returning found that the driveway was blocked. We were unwelcome. When nature's creatures are kicked out, frequently there's nowhere to go. Being good neighbors with them requires knowledge, sometimes changing our actions and accepting them the way they are, other times even utilizing their behaviors to achieve what we want—working smart. That way everyone is happy. And though it was certainly our friend's right to tell us to leave, I believe it is wrong to displace wildlife animals just because we can.

It was late and we had no idea where to go. Linda quickly scanned an old campsite guide as I was driving and discovered a secluded RV park north of town. Jerry and Becky Hill owned Old Mill Run Park, a lovely seasonal trailer park with a Thorntown, Indiana, address. If there are more delightful and understanding people, I'd like to know about them. From the first day we arrived, the Hills were charming and trusting. But our bliss was short-lived, because in three months Old Mill Run Park closed for the winter. Below is a letter Jerry presented to me upon our leaving.

OCTOBER 14, 1993

To Whom It May Concern:

I would like to take this opportunity to introduce Mr. &
Mrs. David Raber and Cougar. David, Linda, and Cougar have
spent the summer with us here at Old Mill Run Park. Of
course, Cougar has been quite the center of attention with all
of our campers. David and Cougar put on a seminar about cat
behavior. The program was originally planned by me for the
children in the campground, but we had as many or more
adults in attendance. Even the residents of our small town have
taken to Cougar.

The reason for this letter is to assure any campground
owner/manager that Cougar's presence in our campground has
been a positive experience. I personally recommend this couple
and their friend to anyone where they might want to stay.

Even though Cougar is a cougar, he is very well behaved
and does not bother anyone. David is very respectful of the
other campers in our park, and never takes Cougar for a walk
if there is a possibility of offending one of the other campers.

We hope that when our campground reopens in the spring
David, Linda, and Cougar will return for the summer.

If you have any questions about Cougar or the Rabers,
please feel free to call me.

Sincerely,

Jerry L. Hill

Owner

This letter didn't mention Regal, because while Cougar,
Linda, and I were in Virginia Beach for the offshore powerboat

grand prix, a little girl spent the entire weekend at the park with Regal and I can only assume she took him home with her, leaving no name or forwarding address. Our only hope is that he is loved, but the pain of not knowing will be daunting forever. Our family was now three.

We moved to a trailer park called CampNothingMuchHere—which is what we wanted. Even without my showing Jerry's letter, Cougar was immediately accepted. Unfortunately, though, a record-breaking, devastatingly cold winter was soon upon us. Not only was snow piled up to the RV's windows, but seventy-five-below-zero wind-chill temperatures were life-threatening in a recreational vehicle. I couldn't walk Cougar for more than ten minutes, fearing his pads might freeze; his urine froze before he was finished; it was impossible to keep fresh water lines and waste water tanks from freezing solid as a rock; the windows remained frosted, and the curtains, if bumped, shattered like glass.

I continued caring for and writing about Cougar, but I could do that anywhere. With a recreational vehicle, I certainly wasn't tied down. But where should we go? The inside of a volcano sounded nice—anywhere warm. At the time, Florida seemed appealing and trailer parks down there were as thick as retirees. I discovered Sherwood Forest trailer park in Palm Harbor, Florida, in a campground book.

SHERWOOD FOREST IS located on the southwest corner of Tampa Road and U.S. Alternate 19, about a half mile from the Gulf of Mexico. Kate was the owner/operator. After several phone conversations with her and establishing that cats were welcome (I didn't go into specifics), Cougar and I headed south in the RV while Linda gave her doctor's office employer two weeks' notice. She would follow.

During Cougar's and my trip, CB radios crackled that a "tiger" was resting in the windshield of a southbound RV. I guess all big cats are considered tigers. In Indiana, 75 percent of the people who met Cougar called him a tiger. And when I asked them where his stripes were, the answer was that he was a female. So, wearily, after a two-day trip, this "tiger" and I reached our destination. The water and sewage tanks, frozen in Indiana, still remained rock solid and the oppressive condensation of living in close quarters, like a dense cold steam, finally escaped out of open windows.

The trailer park office was closed when we arrived. I parked and waited for morning, when I would introduce Cougar. But Cougar didn't want to wait and I can't say that I blamed him. He was ready to get out, stretch his legs, and nose around. So I took him for a walk. Tampa Road and U.S. Alternate 19 is a busy intersection and it wasn't long before he stopped traffic. Kate heard something on the radio about a big cat and thought it interesting, having no idea that they were talking about her new patron. I met her the following morning. By that time she had heard all about Cougar. Thankfully, he was warmly welcomed.

Our stays at a friend's farm, Old Mill Run Park, and CampNothingMuchHere were all in the country, but Sherwood Forest was in Palm Harbor, and people-thick. Taking Cougar for walks twice a day meant walking past at least twenty families, most of whom had dogs and cats. This wasn't what you would call ideal circumstances for a mountain lion, but both Cougar and I learned to live in a densely populated area. We discovered the best times to walk so as not to bother anyone—just as Cougar's wildlife cousins do when people move into their territory.

We lived on a pond, which many ducks and geese also called home. It was a daily routine for Momma Duck and her chicks to waddle out of the water, cross our lawn, and venture into a grassy area across the street. These fowl were very important to Kate, kind of like pets, and had become a signature of the park. My wish for their well-being was twofold: for their sake and mine. It would be easy to point at a dead duck and accuse the largest cat in the neighborhood of the crime, but the only ducks harmed when we lived there were harmed by the paws and jaws of house cats. If Cougar had injured or killed one of those birds, there would have been shouts compared to just whispers complaining about house cats. There's little tolerance for big cats, even when they display exactly the same behavior as house cats. Big is bad, as many people see it. And relative size is the key.

Cougar is too big to catch mice regularly, yet too small to threaten an elephant. Mountain lions don't pursue small animals, but it's not because they are conserving energy, as the "experts" claim. No, it's simply that they have learned that those little beasties are too difficult to catch—it's frustrating watching them scamper away and hide. And cats can be too small to capture certain prey, though some have tried. I remember a picture of a forty-pound lynx holding on to the back of bull moose.

Size has something to do with our being able to safely live in the same territory with mountain lions, but just as important is the fact that we don't fit the picture of their prey. We stand on two legs, not four, confusing their capturing instincts. Of course, it is not advisable to act like children, since screaming and rolling on the ground make us appear smaller and more like a four-legged creature. Nine hundred, ninety-nine thousand, nine hundred and ninety-nine times out of a million everything would be just fine, but why take the chance?

I've learned a great deal about the significance of relative size by watching Cougar's responses to different animals. Cougar is apprehensive of elephants and chooses to walk the other way. He's interested in camels, and he watches them. He observes humans, too, cautiously curious, for our standing vertical makes us threatening. Deer are just about the perfect size and he has a passion for chasing them. He gets a kick out of raccoons, groundhogs, and opossums, but they aren't nearly as exciting as deer. Squirrels are intriguing, but difficult to catch, and the same applies to birds. Field mice will get his attention when he sees them darting about, but they'll just vanish into a hole or crevice, so he's not that interested. He will, however, occasionally trap a chameleon racing over the grass, but only if the lizard is out in the open and easy to catch.

Cougar's hunting isn't prompted by hunger, just entertainment. But he's a cat. His instinctive behavior will be identical to that of wildlife lions hunting for a living. For Cougar, as for all cats, the equation is difficulty versus amusement. When difficulty is greater, a cat will just sit back and look, but when amusement outweighs difficulty, it's time to rock and roll. Beyond that, hunger winds cats up, heightens their emotions. Consequently, the desire to chase changes relative to hunger and how they feel.

So, like us, Cougar is influenced by size. But we are biased. For example, in our society anyone who willingly harms another person is given the legal opportunity to defend himself or prove that his action was justified. Yet when a poor misplaced and hungry cougar kills livestock to survive, then all hell breaks loose. What is an unfortunate cat supposed to do after being run off its territory—lie down and die? Think about it: A poor mother slaughters a neighbor's calf in order to feed herself and her children. Is this poor homeless mother I'm referring to a person or a cat? If she's a person, she is forgiven, maybe even helped. If she's a cat, she'll be shot and her family left to die. And afterward the only question may be why the area is now overrun by deer.

AFTER WE HAD resided at Sherwood Forest for nine months, all the "snowbirds" began migrating south again for the winter. When we had first arrived, the winter season was almost over and the retirees were heading north. Now this place would become a proverbial zoo again. Besides, we all wanted more room. Yes, we had learned to live in a tight place, but I wanted more space and I'm sure Cougar did, too. Timing is everything. We discovered a lovely, Key West–style house in Oldsmar, Florida, at exactly the same time the owner wanted to move out. After we'd lived in the RV for a year and a half, this house seemed palatial: eighteen hundred square feet on stilts, with a wraparound deck overlooking Tampa Bay, a metal roof, and a widow's watch, soon to become a lion's lookout. The owners, Patty and Leo, offered us an option to buy and they loved Cougar living there. The same graciousness and philosophical approach are required to be good neighbors with wildlife. Many profess that wild animals do indeed need more room, but not in their back-yard. Patty and Leo are not that way.

Our next-door neighbors were Tom and Alicia. For the next three and a half years we would live next to these people. They were comfortable and trusting. It wasn't long before Cougar was invited to their pool parties. At one such Fourth of July get-together, several guests were playing with Tom's prized posses-sion, his Notre Dame football. It had resided on the mantel for more than twenty years and was tossed back and forth only on special occasions. One guest underhanded a lob across the pool, and it was intercepted by Cougar. Pop . . . whoosh. Tom was beyond disappointed. Not only did his prized pigskin receive four fang holes, but in all the excitement of his trying to get it out of Cougar's mouth, Cougar tore a hole out of the end and it sank to the bottom of the pool.

There were other adventures. One day, Alicia was watering flowers on her back deck. A stray cat who had preyed on the birds in her outside aviary was passing through our backyard for another snack. This time, Cougar was outside and observing. Cougar, who had never jumped from such heights before, bounded to the top of the deck railing, vaulted to the stair ban-ister, then leapt to the ground, with me racing after him. The stray cat forgot about the birds and took off around Alicia's vine-covered fence, with Cougar following; they both raced around the back, rocketed along the side of the house, around the front, and up the stairs. Alicia heard two muffled thumps as I was doing my best to keep up: the first thump was Cougar, landing halfway up the stairs, then vaulting over the rest of the stairs and over the banister, and ending up on the deck—the second thump. The stray cat skidded around the back corner of the deck and headed for Alicia, who was tending to her flowers. When Alicia looked up, she didn't see the stray. What she did see was Cougar, five feet in the air, heading directly toward her. Before she could blink, Cougar landed at her feet, on top of the stray. Realizing immediately that it was the stray Cougar was after, the same one who had finished off many of her prized birds, she thanked him by lovingly digging her fingers deep into the scruff of his neck. As she did, the stray scooted away, never to be seen again.

Granted, there were some heart-pounding moments, but when all was said and done, everything happened for a reason—a good reason. It's fair to say that Cougar stabilizes neighborhoods, not the reverse. At least there are fewer unwanted strays and petty theft is all but nonexistent. Cougar is respected by all the local police—especially the K-9 contingent. In fact, one time we were awakened at 3 A.M. by police helicopters flying over. Then the phone rang. Apparently two prisoners had escaped while being transported and were thought to be in the vicinity. Since Cougar takes walks twice a day, knows everyone and their pets, and doesn't need a spotlight, they thought he might be able to help locate these characters. They never called back, so I assume they caught the escapees without Cougar's help. Can you imagine the two recognizing that Cougar was following them?

We lived in that place for three and a half years and still I was not in a position to buy the house. Patty and Leo had been patient, but they wanted to sell their house and I couldn't blame them. I even offered to help them find a new buyer, hoping that in the interim I would end up being the one. But when a house-hunting family called for an appointment and came by, they fell in love with the house on the spot, and they required immediate occupancy. We had two days to find another home.

After madly scouring the homes available, we moved several miles away to Safety Harbor. This place, located in a densely populated housing subdivision, was not ideal, but better than nothing. Again, a lease/purchase agreement was signed, but it wasn't that simple. I found myself in the middle of a nasty divorce between the owners. But more important was my exotic animal license. Exotic-animal owners have to be licensed in the state of Florida. We'd had to move from Oldsmar in two days, less time than it would take to mail the appropriate forms, so I called the authorities to let them know of our move. A secretary thanked me and typed my new address into the computer.

Not long afterwards there was a television special regarding a tiger circus mishap and I was interviewed as the expert on big cats. The television network got my name, address, and telephone number from the Florida Game and Fresh Water Fish Commission, the agency I had called and informed of my new address. But more about that later.

Things were looking up for us financially and buying this home was just around the corner, but the battling owners had declared World War Three. The wife said she had the authority to sign a six-month lease/purchase agreement without the signature of her ex, but after we moved in, her ex-husband wanted his money now. The wife stated that the air-conditioning system was new. It was actually twenty years old and it expired the day we moved in. She agreed to pay for half of a replacement unit, then stopped payment on her check. After six months of this, it was time to move once again. Wildlife, unfortunately, don't have that luxury.

A REAL ESTATE agent named Teresa found us a home in Tarpon Springs, Florida, a sleepy Greek village anchoring its economy in fishing, sponging, and tourism. Teresa's "find" was located fifty yards from the Gulf of Mexico, overlooking Howard Park. It looked like our long-lost home at last. Ron and Donna, the owners, were proud that a "celebrity" cat was moving in, and they were going to build a larger home next door and be our neighbors. Everything was coming up roses—but roses have thorns.

Ron was a gabber and told everyone about Cougar. It wasn't long before three Tarponites were opposed to the idea of a big cat moving into the neighborhood and they turned up the heat and stirred the pot. Sensationalism turns people into a mob. Mobs don't think objectively, they just react to an artificial alarm, stirred up by misplaced souls who get their power through lack of knowledge, misunderstanding, misrepresenting and misjudging. This scenario could also describe someone not wishing to live in proximity to a wildlife cat.

I believe that knowledge and courtesy go a long way to establish comfort in a unique situation. But unfortunately Ron had "let the cat out of the bag" without my being able to address any questions from the neighbors. So these three objectors organized an anti-Cougar campaign. Eventually there were announcements over the schools' PA system about a ferocious cat moving to Tarpon Springs; the announcements gave Ron and Donna's children's address, in order to put pressure on the entire family not to sell their house to us. Signs picturing an angry cat inside a circle with a slanted line were handed out on school property.

Then there were city council meetings where I was told that even though we had the legal right to move to Tarpon Springs, officials couldn't guarantee our safety. Imagine being told that you can move, but at your own risk. Suddenly, I knew what wildlife cats endure. For me it was like being mad at the wind, the tenacious whisper of misunderstanding, until a bullet changes your life, maybe even takes it.

During a city council meeting the mayor of Tarpon Springs asked me just one question: "How long are Cougar's teeth?" The mayor was utilizing sensationalism, the same stuff that motivates gangs. She never checked with my former neighbors—or any former mayors, for that matter. The Oldsmar mayor, past whose house Cougar and I had walked every day for three and a half years, called me and said, "David, you can't fight ignorance."

And many former neighbors, hearing about my problem, voluntarily showed up at the Tarpon Springs city council meetings, offering their support. This was embarrassing enough without the story being all over the evening news. A reporter showed up at the front door of our present house in Safety Harbor where we had resided for six months, but after seeing a sign saying

WELCOME HOME QUADRUPLETS on my next-door neighbor's house, she and the cameraman ran over and knocked on the door. When it opened, the reporter, with camera whirling, asked what it was like living next door to a mountain lion, especially with four newborns. My neighbor said that she had no idea that a big cat lived next door, that we were quiet, respectful, and great neighbors. "Big cat," she remarked, staring at the camera, "so what?"

Some get the picture and others don't. This is not unlike being neighbors with wildlife cats. Get rid of sensationalism and so what? These big cats want nothing more than to be left alone and will even change their habits so as not to be seen. Face it, you are safer sharing territory with wildlife cats than going to school. When a youngster brings a gun to class, does that mean we should eliminate classrooms? Of course not; schools are too important. We should learn why youngsters behave that way and try to prevent the incident from happening again. Wildlife cats are important, too. We should learn about them. Without knowing them, there still have only been twelve human fatalities caused by mountain lions in the last hundred years. That's safer than drinking milk. Should we try to sanitize the world by eliminating large cats and problem children, or is it better to understand them and learn to minimize the risk, whether it be at school or in the woods?

Tarpon Springs taught me a lot. I now understood bigotry, prejudice, and discrimination. The Florida Game and Fresh Water Fish Commission showed up at my door, accusing me of not informing them of my current address. Remember, I had not utilized the standard form because of time, relying instead on the telephone. Also remember that the Game Commission knew where I was, since they gave my address and telephone number to the television network for the television special on the tiger circus mishap. But now two officers were threatening to take Cougar. I said they would have to take me, too: I would not be separated from him. After several hours of talking on their car radios and trying to decide what to do, they cited me for not filling out the proper paperwork—a criminal misdemeanor.

I have learned that the Florida Game and Fresh Water Fish Commission placates people where as the USDA, my federal licensing agency, aids the animal.

When I showed up in court the judge asked, "What are you doing here?"

I answered, "Your Honor, I really don't know."

He shook his head, thought for a moment, then asked, "Are you familiar with the PTI program?"

"No, Your Honor."

"Go downstairs to Room 115 and talk to Stacie."

PTI is short for pretrial intervention. Essentially, if you don't make the same mistake again for six months, the case is thrown out. Given the alternative of fighting the three connected Tarponites who politically brought this on me, I grudgingly thought it wise to accept the judge's offer. During the six-month PTI program the "accused" has to show up once a month, pay fifty dollars, and leave. At my first visit I was told that I need not return, just mail in my three hundred dollars. I hate to lose, especially when I've tried to do everything right, but it takes money to fight back, money I didn't have.

BUT EVERYTHING HAPPENS for a reason. While going through this ordeal and still living in Safety Harbor, I found the ideal waterfront home, next door to five acres of big-cat running room and oak trees draped with Spanish moss. The house was more cottagelike, with 3,200 square feet of *mine* on the water, overlooking an inlet of Old Tampa Bay. And across the water was Upper Tampa Bay Park, where several families of bald eagles lived. From my back deck it was difficult to see another house; it was a place for perspective. This neighborhood could be described as horsey; there are several stables within half a mile. Most important, the Florida Game and Fresh Water Fish Commission inspected the property prior to our moving and approved it with flying colors.

Pat and Judy live across the street on a canal with three cats and Shala, the most amiable German shepherd in existence. Shala's name comes from a Lakota Indian name, Haya Washula, meaning wolf sister. Shala is the outdoor type, spending her entire day with Pat, who owns a company that mitigates and restores wetlands. Early in the morning Pat drives to work in his truck and Shala sits in the passenger seat, looking through the windshield, just like Pat. When Pat readies his boat, Shala waits. When Pat works out back, Shala observes. Shala is Pat and Pat is Shala.

Shala and Cougar have a common interest—squirrels. If Cougar is out stalking, Shala will wait and watch, observe Cougar patiently stalking until she just can't control herself, and start, rushing and barking. Granted, Shala is never successful at capturing squirrels, but she sure has fun failing.

Pat and Judy are in tune with animals. But there are some people who profess to be animal sympathizers and really are not.

Our neighbors next door, Mike and Barbara, have four parrots and two dogs, Bullet and Bugger. Mike and Barbara believe their dogs can do no wrong. Consequently, any problems, such as roaming, eliminating, or barking, are not their problem.

During Cougar's walks Bugger and Bullet bark incessantly. And I'm convinced barking is a canine language that Cougar interprets. The other neighborhood dogs will bark a hello, whereas Bugger and Bullet bark obscenities. There are times when their barking lasts from 6:30 A.M. until 11:00 P.M. And as if auditory abuse weren't enough, they madly circle our home every day, causing Cougar to fly from window to window. I asked Mike and Barbara to corral their canines. But my request fell on deaf ears: Mike and Barbara viewed my complaint as my problem, not theirs. After all, they said, dogs will be dogs.

One day Cougar and I came out for a walk and I saw Bugger and Bullet eliminating in my backyard as Barbara worked in her garden. I didn't like the barking. I didn't like the running around my house. And I didn't like the unwanted fertilizer. I released the pressure on Cougar's leash, allowing him to advance toward Bugger and Bullet as they sniffed what they had left on my lawn. I thought Cougar's presence would cause them to vacate the premises, but I was wrong. They didn't run, but rushed Cougar. I didn't want a fight, so as I was facing the dogs, I pulled Cougar around close to me, corralling his head and neck between my legs. Both dogs started biting at his flank. If I let Cougar go, we'd have a free-for-all. If I continued to restrain him, the dogs could injure him. It was like separating your youngster and the town bully, both of whom want to fight.

I yelled a low-pitched command that seemed to come from my toes. The dogs looked up. With me restraining Cougar, I seemed to be their only threat. I stared at them, knowing full well that I'd break both of their necks with my bare hands if they harmed Cougar. They backed away. Then I yelled at Barbara to restrain her dogs. Mike heard the commotion from his deck and shouted that I shouldn't walk Cougar until his dogs were back inside. Funny, I didn't realize that I had to schedule Cougar's walking on his own property around his dogs' agenda, so I briskly took Cougar back to the house and returned for further discussion.

Barbara and Mike felt they were due an apology. Granted, I did raise my voice. They said their dogs were just doing what is natural. I agreed. They said that I was an animal person and shouldn't object to their dogs, which brings me back to one of my goals: Be good neighbors with wildlife. But being a good neighbor depends on mutual respect.

Mike and Barbara called the Florida Game and Fresh Water Fish Commission to complain, admitting that they would withdraw their objection if I apologized for yelling. I didn't know they had called. But even if I had, I felt that I had done nothing wrong. I was, after all, *legally* walking Cougar on my *approved* property. But guess again.

Earlier, when I was inspected for this new home, my inspector had informed me of a new regulation requiring five-foot perimeter fencing, designed to keep intruders out, not animals in. He said that a fence was a matter of interpretation; it could be any type of barrier between my property and the public. He nodded toward the water, pointed to the vegetation at the front of my property and to a four-foot dilapidated fence, not on my property but along the vacant lot next to me, and said they would suffice. In retrospect, I believe my inspector respected me and eased the interpretation of a formal perimeter fence. My property was approved, perimeter fence and all. But after a complaint, trust me, everything changes.

There are two hands at the commission, the one at the state capital and the one in the field. The Tallahassee hand said that I didn't have a perimeter fence, and my inspector, seemingly without realizing that he was implicating himself, cited me for not having one in the formal sense—a criminal offense. Given the wavering nature of my inspector, I wonder how safe wildlife really are.

I have a Florida exhibitor's license, which means that I can "exhibit" Cougar—take him anywhere I deem safe without the aid of perimeter fencing. This is confusing. I can walk Cougar downtown in a crowd without any barriers, but I am required to have a fence while walking him at home. It doesn't make sense.

The court agreed that I was unfairly accused, but that still didn't address the formal interpretation of a five-foot perimeter fence. So it was agreed that I would erect a fence and all charges would be dropped. But for Cougar and me a five-foot fence is dangerous. First of all, a fence would be like a neon sign illuminating exactly where Cougar lived, at a height that any youngster could climb, a height that Cougar could easily vault but that would be impassable for me. So I chose a ten-foot fence. Cougar could roam off his lead, and all uninvited guests would be kept at bay.

Ironically, Cougar now has more freedom with a fence than without. This is something like what could be applied to being good neighbors with wildlife. In a wildlife scenario big cats don't wish to visit towns, there's no cover, and no one serves deer on the hoof. But the cats *could* visit. So there could be fenced-in areas surrounding playgrounds where kids could be kids without Mom or Dad worrying about something happening that is much more unlikely than a lightning strike. Yes, it takes a little precaution sharing this planet with wildlife, sometimes just stopping to think.

For example, in Tampa, Florida, several years ago there were abnormally large numbers of vultures circling high overhead. No one really had an explanation or saw any of them touch down, but complaints did land. However, before drastic measures were taken, these soaring scavengers, who clean up hundreds of wildlife road casualties every day, moved on.

It's not man versus wildlife, but man with wildlife.

7

THROUGH THEIR EYES

WHAT SHOULD WE do before trying to help someone? The answer is to relate, crawl into that person's skin and find out what makes him or her tick. Only then can we help. It's no different with cats, but understanding them frequently means stepping away from our world and entering theirs.

Our world doesn't look, hear, smell, taste, or feel the same as it does for felines. Wear infrared night goggles, a high-powered sound dish, amplify your sense of smell a hundredfold, numb your skin, then get an attitude. Now you're relating. It all feels rather exotic, but understanding cats without this correlation is impossible.

The most difficult feline detail for us to understand is their sense of smell. Our noses just don't work nearly as well, and cats are scent-driven. Eighty percent of their behavior occurs because their nose says so. We, on the other hand, are sight-driven. So if we see a cat doing something, we explain it visually, which is why there is so much misunderstanding about cats—like saying cats are sharpening their claws when, in fact, they're scenting. Or that they're cleaning themselves when, many times, they're scenting. Or that they're urinating when, many times, they're scenting. Or saying that some cats love to be petted when, in fact, they immediately wash the objectionable scents away. It's impossible to know exactly how a cat perceives the world, but we can get close. So let's start with what's most important to us: sight.

Cougar's favorite color is red, his second favorite is blue, and his third favorite is green, but bright colors take priority; a flashy yellow is more enticing to him than a dull red. I first learned this when he was walking beside a long string of outdoor Christmas lights. He'd stop and sniff the red lights every time, sniff the blue ones most times, check out the green ones less frequently, and bypass the others. Then, while walking through woods where trees were marked with equally bright plastic ribbons, he always investigated the red tags, seldom missed the blue ones, examined the green ones occasionally, and walked past tags of other colors.

But color for Cougar is only the background; the foreground is motion. Experts say cats see hundreds of times better than we, but that depends on the type of object seen. Remember, when one of an animal's senses is especially acute in one area, then that sense will be compromised in other areas. You never get something for nothing; there is always a sacrifice for acuteness.

Take a motionless, brightly colored bug sitting two feet under your cat's nose. You can see it better than your cat. He sees only a lightly colored blur and may even miss it entirely. Now have that bug crawl up a distant wall. It's too small for you to see, but your cat will zero in on it, because it's moving. Motion is vastly more important to a cat than color.

A cat is able to assimilate many moving bits and mentally glue them together into an entire picture, such as a mouse darting through the underbrush. What is just a blur of tiny little pieces to us is seen as an entire mouse by the cat. And that mosaic is accurate enough for the cat to tell if the mouse is looking at him or not.

An example of this was when Cougar and I were walking along a four-foot-high, three-foot-thick hedgerow. Two dogs where on the other side. As we walked, I could look over the bushes, getting an unobstructed view of the dogs and they of me, whereas Cougar could only peer through the exceptionally dense leaves and branches. The dogs were unaware of Cougar. I was amazed that Cougar could not only see where the dogs were, but would stop walking every time either of them looked our way. I got down on his level and could see only occasional flecks of motion. Cougar was able to organize all those flecks into an entire animal, even to the point of knowing the animal was looking his way.

Then there was the time when Cougar stopped after discovering a rabbit in thick grass. From my vantage point I could see that the rabbit was looking directly at us. But when I got down on Cougar's level, the rabbit all but disappeared, completely obscured by grass, so I stood up again. When the rabbit turned his head, Cougar rushed forward. Where I could see little to nothing, Cougar could see eyes or at the very least head position.

Have you ever laughed seeing a cat hide behind a leaf? It's funny watching a cat trying to conceal his entire body behind something much smaller. Is that cat dumb? Absolutely not. The truth of the matter is that the cat is just hiding his eyes. Animals consider that if you are looking away, you're not interested. We can watch a pride of lions walk down to the water hole past their prey, and though the prey animals' demeanor is guarded, they do not run. That's because the lions aren't looking at them.

The same thing applies to a swishing tail. Why in the world does a cat swish his tail when it might scare away the very animal he's trying to catch? Is he too excited to control his tail? Hardly. It's a diversion. The cat doesn't want to let on that he's staring. In the animal world, a thrashing tail has little significance, but a stare means everything. The intended prey is distracted by the movement of the tail and doesn't see eyes staring at it. Cats aren't the only animals to move their tails as a diversion. How about squirrels?

How many times have you caught your cat off guard? Maybe you're wearing an unfamiliar hat or have just changed your clothes. Your cat doesn't recognize you until he gets a whiff of you or hears your voice, because his visual image of you isn't that clear. It's the same reason why Cougar leaves nose smudges on windows. I'm sure he doesn't enjoy bumping his nose. He simply can't see where the glass is and advances until he bumps into it.

And how about cats, and dogs for that matter, running into chain-link fences when they are chasing something. The fence is apparent to us but almost invisible to the cat. I explain this as being similar to our putting on a pair of dirty sunglasses. The dirt becomes almost invisible as we see through the lenses to whatever it is that we're looking at.

Recognizing that Cougar's visual acuity is not as good as mine, I rarely pass him without extending my hand and allowing him to sniff. It's a matter of courtesy, helping him recognize me. And I never come through the door without bending down and letting him sniff whatever it is that I'm carrying. Again, just a matter of courtesy. And when returning after eating, I always bend down so Cougar can sniff my mouth, letting him know what I have eaten.

Let's try to visually relate to Cougar and all cats by turning down the lights. Colors become dull and sharp edges become less distinct. Now we too would miss that colorful bug up close, unless it were moving. We too would be frightened if approached because we're not able to see who's coming. Welcome to the cat's world. So cats don't see as well as we when it's bright, but when it's dark, the balance flips in their favor. We can hardly see a thing in the darkness, while the cat is able to pick up distinct shadows, and because movement is so critical, any shadow that moves stands out.

The physiology of the cat's eye helps us understand all of this. House cats' eyes, pupils, and lenses are proportionally larger than those of other carnivores; their pupils are able to open to an area three times larger than our own, allowing more light to be focused on the retina. As a matter of fact, larger eyes relative to the size of their head normally indicates that an animal has superior night vision. House cats are nocturnal, but mountain lions are crepuscular (active in twilight). The house cat's vertical pupil can open wider and close tighter than the round pupil of a mountain lion (or a human), enabling him to both shut out light when it's too bright and gather light when the illumination level is low. But there is always a downside to specialization. It's my belief that this vertical pupil also doesn't produce as sharp an image on the retina as a round one would. (I've never seen a camera with an elliptical lens; the lenses are all round.) So with a round pupil the mountain lion has a slightly sharper image and is suited best for dusk and dawn, while the house cat sacrifices a slight visual acuity for the ability to see better at night.

Our retina is composed of cones for seeing color and rods for night vision. Not surprisingly, cats have more rods and fewer centrally oriented cones than we do; this suggests that their color vision is not as vivid as ours. Behind the cat's retina is a layer of reflective cells called the tapetum lucidum, responsible for reflecting light back through the retina; this gives them almost twice the amount of light that we have available. It is what causes the characteristic eye shine we see when cats are illuminated by headlights or a flashlight pointing their way. Animals displaying this characteristic have these specialized reflective cells for seeing better at night. Animals freeze in the bright headlights of an approaching car, but we don't. Why? Bright light temporarily blinds us both, but animals fear only what they perceive and, for the moment, there is nothing to worry about.

We can't leave sight without discussing what happens in the blink of an eye. Of course, we all recognize that when cats are interested their eyes are wide open and they don't blink; in essence, they are saying that they don't want to miss anything. But there are other times when they do blink, and this is like a cooing smile. When Cougar blinks it relays that he is fond, comfortable, affectionate, and caring. I began blinking back and discovered that blinking softened my stare. I could still see, but I trusted everything would be okay. That's the meaning of a blink, and the duration means something, too. A short blink means "I like you" and a longer blink conveys a higher level of trust, just as for humans. Who says we are not instinctual.

Now let's take a *look* (sight bias) at hearing. A cat would have wanted to take a *smell* at hearing. But back to audio. Experts speculate that cats hear, as well as see, much better than we do, and again they must be more specific. When it comes to sounds in the ultrasonic range, cats do indeed hear much better than we, but we can hear bass sounds better. By observing the sounds that a cat reacts to, we can better understand how he hears.

Take those cars loaded with high-powered amplifiers and huge speakers pounding out bass so loud you can feel them thumping blocks away. Cougar doesn't hear them, doesn't even flick an ear in their direction. I've observed Cougar around all sorts of noises and noticed that, in every case, low-frequency sounds get little to no response.

Increase the frequency a little and we get to growling and snarling noises. Low-frequency sounds like these are negative, implying that a fight is possible. We instinctively talk low when we're angry, and so does the cat. But, interestingly, when we flutter or pulsate low-frequency sounds, they turn positive, like our cooing or cats' purring. This is similar to what blinking does to a stare.

Increase the frequency a little more and we get to the mid-range frequency of the human voice. These are neutral noises. When Cougar chirps in the midrange he's just saying hello, nothing really important, like most of our talking.

Increase the frequency a little more and we get to a high-pitched human voice. We instinctively talk in high tones when something is cute and cuddly, suggesting that everything is am-icable and friendly. This is the same tone the cat uses when mating. But if we intensify a high-pitched sound it reverses in meaning and becomes a scream. A scream is the only noise by an unknown human that gets Cougar's attention, and the same applies to us. A shrill scream will always turn a person's head. Cougar is apathetic to all other human noises, unless they're mine. When Cougar and I are walking at night I might hear what I would consider a suspicious sound, like someone clearing his throat, but Cougar could care less. He does, however, know his name. If someone who he doesn't know calls his name, Cougar looks up.

We then move to a little higher-frequency sound like a hiss, or the snapping of a twig, or the rustling of leaves. This is the range where Cougar is particularly well suited. Cougar can hear a field mouse darting in grass fifteen feet away, and I believe that just by listening, he can distinguish how many mice there are.

How many times have you "silently" walked around the corner of your carpeted hallway only to discover that your cat knew you were coming. But how? Some say telepathy. Maybe . . . but he also heard you. You may think you are making no noise, but the carpet and pad make high-pitched snapping noises when compressed. And don't forget the high-pitched noise that the tips of your shoelaces make in tapping the tops of your shoes. And how about the sound of your joints? The older you are, the more noise you make. Bones moving against cartilage make sounds that cats can hear.

One of the most alluring sounds for Cougar is a human sneeze or someone blowing his nose, which to us sounds similar to the cat's hiss. But the sneeze and the hiss sound different enough to convey opposite meanings for cats. The sneeze and nose-blowing lack the intensity of a hiss.

This is not unlike spoken language, like Chinese, where intonation changes the meaning. Nature's language isn't quite so complicated. Take the hiss of a cat and the rattle of a rattlesnake; these have similar high-pitched sounds with the same translation: BACK OFF! Both high-intensity sounds.

Actually, cats and other animals communicate very well without words. Words, after all, can be misleading, sometimes even deceitful. There's nothing deceptive about a hiss, and around the world cats never need an interpreter or a translator. Not only is their language universal, but other animals understand them, too.

Then we move to the ultrasonic range. Boating in the Gulf of Mexico, Cougar will hang his head over the side and seemingly stare at the surface of the water. There's nothing visible as he moves his head back and forth. Then a porpoise will break the surface. Cougar is listening to the high-pitched whistles of the porpoises. His head follows them; he scans with his ears. When they break the surface, he is looking directly at them and he excitedly nudges me to make sure I see them, too. It all starts when he'll be snoozing in the boat and will look up when I have heard nothing. I believe a boat becomes an antenna for sounds underwater. I remember hearing distant motorboats speeding around the lake, their sounds amplified by the boat I was in. It is my belief that Cougar will hear an underwater sound intensified by the boat hull, then hang his head over the side to locate its exact position.

Not only is Cougar able to effectively capture sounds by

pointing his ears in the direction of the noise, the hair immediately in front and to the side of his ears grows in distinct lines, helping to channel noises into his ear canal. So cutting or altering the hair in front of a cat's ear will impede his hearing, not help it.

And what about their sense of touch? Cats vary from acutely sensitive to mildly so. The tip of the nose and the paws are more sensitive than the skin. The skin of a cat is much thicker and tougher than ours, having a lesser nerve supply. Can you imagine a cat racing through the brush with skin as sensitive as ours? Yes, cats' fur helps protect against scrapes and scratches, but even without that protection, their skin is not as sensitive to stimulation as ours. As I mentioned earlier, if one area of a particular sense is weak, albeit for good reason, there will be another area to compensate. Whiskers, for the cat, are this balance, his tactile superiority. The cat is able to use whiskers as we do fingers, without the threat of getting burned, for like our hair, they are not heat sensitive.

I remember a television program telling me that whiskers are located around the nose to allow a cat to run full speed ahead, dart through a small opening, and know if his body can make it through without getting stuck. In all my observations, I've never seen that happen. If that were the main reason for whiskers, then it would make sense that they should grow longer as the cat puts on weight, but they don't. How about fat cats, do they get stuck? And what about mountain lions and cheetahs, who have small heads in proportion to their bodies. They'd get squeezed every time if they relied on their whiskers. No, whiskers, in fact, surround the business end of a cat. He needs to feel his prey when administering the coup de grâce, and since he is so dependent on his nose, it makes perfect sense to surround this most important sense organ with an accurate means to explore what he's smelling. Especially one impervious to the bites and swipes of prey and adversaries.

I was lecturing on how the movement of whiskers is revealing, saying it indicates a cat's level of interest. Whiskers next to the cat's face indicates little to no concern, whereas sticking straight forward indicates fully heightened attention. A woman in the audience, having had cats her entire life, said she was unaware that whiskers even moved. But indeed they do. Cougar will even have one side of his whiskers pointing straight forward, indicating that he is excited, and at the same time pull the other side back against his face, because I'm approaching on that side and he doesn't wish to bump me with them. And when I'm racing him up the stairs, his whiskers on the other side of me will be forward, indicating that he's excited, while the whiskers next to me will be against his face so as not to be stubbed against my legs.

Cats' toes have thickened undersides called pads. These pads aren't nearly as sensitive as our fingertips, but then we don't normally walk on our hands. Cougar's pads are extremely sensitive to temperature, though. As he's walking along on a hot day, Cougar pays particular attention to the temperature of the ground. When he steps on a cool place, he plops down to cool off. And something else . . .

Cougar's heel pads have a unique shape. They look identical

to the stealth bomber, a fact that is interesting to me. Our government spends billions of dollars developing a stealthy shape when all its engineers had to do was look at a cat's paw and mimic what has been stealthy for millions of years. And just like an airplane, Cougar's paws are strong, but delicate. He can jump down, comfortably crushing his paws under the weight of his two hundred pounds dropping twenty feet, but if I high-five slapped his paw, he would limp for days.

Before leaving the sense of touch I'd like to bring up temperature. What temperature (in degrees Fahrenheit) is Cougar the most comfortable with, and when is he too hot or cold? Cougar likes it in the sixties, while the fifties are a little chilly and the nineties a little warm. But temperature isn't as simple as looking at a thermometer. There is a difference between inside and outside temperature.

When Cougar is in front of an audience, I want him to be comfortable, just as always. If the temperature climbs past seventy-four degrees, he will get up and leave. He knows that in his car the air conditioner is blasting in preparation for him. But when he is outside, eighty-five degrees and warmer is comfortable. There's something uncomfortable about confinement and it's not just the humidity, because many times it's very humid when he's comfortably walking outside in the eighties. I believe attention has something to do with it. When outside, his mind is occupied as he walks, so he ignores the fact that he's slightly warm or cold, and moving helps. Similarly, when we are working in a classroom the temperature has to be cooler to be acceptable than the temperature outside when we are walking.

And confinement makes Cougar guarded. If he were eating

out in the middle of the room, he'd be comfortable. But if he were in the corner or down the hall, somewhere he is hemmed in, he'd start to growl if anyone but me approached. And towering over him makes him uncomfortable compared to being on his level. So any attempt to take something that he is possessive of should always be done out in the open and on his level.

Cougar, like all cats, could very well have a sixth sense, but most of his behaviors can be explained by just knowing how he sees, hears, and touches his surroundings. It's difficult to relate, but we can understand night vision, high-pitched noises, and whiskers. However, our nose is comparatively so miserably impotent that it's almost impossible to correlate to a cat's ability to smell and the importance scent plays in his life. When we don't understand, frequently irritation is the result, but we must fight back those feelings and try to understand the real reasons why our cats do the things they do. Take my couch, for example.

I had driven a rental automobile home while Cougar's Suburban was being serviced. I then sat on my couch and eventually got up. Cougar didn't like the smell of whoever had sat in the rental car and took care of it—his way. He bit the perfect image of my seat out of the cushion.

I question the experts when they say that dogs have a better sense of smell than cats. We all know cats smell better—after all, they clean themselves regularly. Seriously, concerning the sense of smell, I believe the experts are wrong again. They lecture that dogs have longer noses, with fifty square inches of olfactory cells compared to six square inches for a cat. And they say that because the brain of a dog has 5 percent set aside for smelling compared to 3 percent for a cat, the dog's sense of smell is keener. But I say not so fast. If the ability to smell relied solely on sensor or brain cell numbers they might be right, without considering the possibility that a cat's olfactory sensors could be more sensitive than a dog's. But only cats have Jacobson's organs. Right behind the two front teeth in the roof of every cat's mouth are two little holes leading to these ancient organs. Humans used to have them, but now they are not operational, residing only as remnants in the roofs of our mouths. These organs turbo-charge the cat's ability to "see" a scent. "Flehming" and "grimacing" are the terms used to describe the cat's behavior when Jacobson's organs have shifted into high gear. Cougar will dab the tip of his tongue on something especially interesting and salivate to moisten, lifting the scent; then he will tilt his head back, sticking his tongue out and down with his ears flat, horizontal to the ground. Then, imperceptibly, he will inhale, guiding this scent up over his tongue, up into the roof of his mouth. He's in heaven. Cougar, like all cats, enjoys the magnificence of a scent like a present-day art connoisseur enjoys viewing a Rembrandt or a van Gogh. And just as when we're not visually appreciating something, we still can see, a cat not displaying flehming is still using his Jacobson's organs. These organs are always working. When a dog sniffs the air for scents, his mouth is closed, but Cougar's mouth is frequently open. He's not just using his nose, he's also using his tongue and Jacobson's organs.

Dogs may have the ability to better capture airborne scents, but when it comes to lifting a particular scent off of something, I give cats the nod. Cougar will be walking outside and suddenly his nose dives for the ground and he prods, exploring the scent of urine left behind by him or another animal. If you're a car nut, you'll understand when I say that it's like a Lamborghini Diablo screeching to a halt in front of you. Cougar meticulously checks out the scent, just like you would the car.

And when it's time to defecate, Cougar has to find the perfect place. He searches until he discovers a musty smell, like that of wet leaves. And when finished, he will bury his feces with debris. Why? People, being sight driven, say he does so to cover it, obstruct it from view, but that's not the case. It wouldn't make sense that he would shift gears after depending on his sense of smell to now be concerned with how the feces looks. No, he's disguising the scent. By scooping the ground saturated with the musty scent that drew him there in the first place, he is obscuring the smell of his feces—camouflaging the scent—for the sake of stealth. How do I know? If he were visually covering, he'd look at what he's doing; but he doesn't. He continuously sniffs, meticulously checking the smell. But it doesn't end there.

The smell of feces is appealing to Cougar for the first three days. Then the signature alters, changes to something negative, something to avoid. For three days Cougar on walks will check where he has defecated, but around the fourth day he steers clear. And if he should happen to walk past the same place weeks later, he will literally jump out of the way. This is the reason, I believe, why animals sometimes use feces to mark their territory, for after several days the feces literally push animals back, even when it's their own. The scent of urine is just the opposite: it's a come-on, an invitation. Cougar never backs away from either his or another animal's urine trail.

During a walk Cougar will usually "take care of business,"

cover it, then walk on. But inevitably he will circle back to check the smell from a different perspective, approaching from a different direction, the way we might view a picture on the wall from different angles. In other words, he wishes to remain incognito and wants to make sure his scent is covered from every direction.

After checking into a hotel Cougar will immediately nose around to check out the room. He will eventually find a spot where a dog or cat has been, maybe even using flehming for a keen sense of it. That's where I place his tray—the place where previous animals thought the bathroom was and where Cougar agrees. Eventually, when Cougar wants to eliminate, he'll walk over to that spot and use his tray. Is he housebroken? Kind of. If I were to place his tray where I think it should be, using sight rather than smell, he would use it 75 percent of the time; the other 25 percent, he would saunter over to where the animals go—and go.

Scratching, or "sharpening claws," also depends on scenting. Cougar will never walk up to, look at, and drag his paws over something (remember he is declawed). No, he approaches nose first, checks out the scent, and only then goes through the exact same behavior as cats with claws. And it's not surprising that he goes through the identical motions as a clawed cat, because claws have little to do with the behavior. Cats have scent glands in their paws and are attracted to something that smells good. Like, "Why not freshen up a bit? . . . I'll just put my scent here for others to notice and wear that perfume on my paws."

We know certain scents attract cats—scents like urine, newspaper, wood, and that Bitter Apple stuff you buy to keep them away from your couch and chair. Negative scents are more difficult to discover and smearing old discarded feces on the arm of your couch just wouldn't do, so let's utilize a lesson from Pavlov and his dogs. Since cats don't like hissing noises, spray a fragrance that you like around your cat. The experience will not be pleasant for him. Do this several times until your cat connects the fragrance with the hissing. Now spray this fragrance on the arm of the couch where he has been scratching. Your cat will associate this fragrance with the unpleasant experience of the hissing noise and choose to scratch elsewhere. But where? Cats love the smell of wood. Rub a twig or piece of wood on whatever it is you want your cat to scratch.

There are scents that Cougar despises—onion and garlic. If I want him to move, an onion works wonders. Normally, I don't even have to put it under his nose, for just by getting into the refrigerator, opening the drawer where the makings for salads are kept and approaching him with this objectionable bulb is enough to make him get up and move. Garlic has the same effect times ten.

While Cougar is walking, an airborne scent will get his attention: he'll turn, sniffing with his mouth open, and walk in its direction. I'm positive this same technique is used by his wildlife cousins for hunting. Ten feet away, Cougar can smell a squirrel hiding on the other side of a tree. But as I said before, cats can smell a scent better when they are able to dab their tongue on it.

There has never been a time walking on a trail that Cougar has not stopped to sniff the little branches and twigs along the way, for they have scraped along the sides of passing animals and people. Just by observing how high the scent is from the ground, I get an excellent idea of what is in front of us. If Cougar reaches high to sniff, it's a person or deer. If he sniffs low, it's probably a raccoon or possum. Eventually, we'll run into whoever it is that he's tracking. Both people and animals use trails. Seldom, if ever, has Cougar followed a scent through thick foliage.

And Cougar can smell things that we would consider imperceptible. For example, after it has snowed he can follow my car by smelling its tracks in the snow. After discovering this, I thought I'd confirm my suspicions by driving my four-wheel-drive vehicle over a well-traveled remote road and field and summoning Cougar for a walk. He followed my car tracks without fail. Later I watched the owner of the campground padlock a gate. Rain or shine, for eight weeks Cougar would check his scent on the lock. That's two months later!

Taste is tricky. There's no picture, sound, or smell, but taste is indeed closely related to fragrances. Cats aren't wild about vegetables or fruit because, after all, they are carnivores. But Cougar loves a certain type of grass—like crabgrass with tassels—sometimes called wheat grass. He munches on it every day without fail. Since we usually walk after Cougar eats, everything stays down. But if Cougar eats grass on an empty stomach then he vomits. I think this is nature's way of helping out during sickness. Cats like to eat grass. Healthy cats are eating food. Cats with physical problems don't eat food, but because of their love for grass, they'll always munch some, which, on an empty stomach, will make them vomit, possibly remedying their sickness. People who view cats eating grass say that they are willingly trying to vomit, but I don't think that's the case. They always eat grass and vomit only if they eat it when their stomachs are empty.

Cougar will play with and chew on bananas but never swallow them. And since I have always fed him by hand, it is easy to notice something very important. Before Cougar takes a bite of anything, he dabs it with his tongue, like a quick-check, using taste buds, nose, and Jacobson's organs, before he snatches and swallows. Cats are known to be finicky eaters and I believe it's because of this triad of closely related sensory receptors. With such an acute sense of taste, it's too bad that cats' teeth are designed only for ripping and tearing, not for chewing. But then I'm thinking human; maybe their sense of taste is so sensitive that they receive plenty of pleasure just by swallowing something whole. And because dogs, compared to cats, pay no attention to what they eat, should we say the reason is that cats have more taste?

8

MEDICAL MATTERS MEAN MENTAL, TOO

DO YOU BELIEVE that your mental well-being can influence your physical health? How about the reverse? With animals, we can readily see their physical problems, but their psychological troubles may be less conspicuous.

Sometimes the slogan "if it ain't broke, don't fix it" is appropriate, but there's a problem regarding felines. It's difficult to tell if they're broken or not. When they finally act sick, they could be on their ninth life, so it is important to "fix" them before it's too late.

And just as important, if not more so, is preventing them from getting sick or injured in the first place. Diabetes has taught me to work at being healthy. There's nothing to lose and everything to gain. I don't take good health for granted and I will never take depressing prognoses lying down. Caring for cats is no different, and wanting to get well plays an important part in recovery. And for big cats there is another problem: treatment can be complicated.

After returning home from our time in the Florida Keys, Cougar became ill. He just lay in the corner with his nose warm and dry and didn't eat or drink. Peter Veling was Cougar, Chivas, and Regal's veterinarian, and his office was just a half mile away. Peter had seen Cougar for check-ups and vaccinations, but nothing serious until this illness. The following is Peter's account not only of treating Cougar but of his reflections, after ten years of introspection:

> As Cougar's first doctor I have been fortunate to watch Cougar, David, and Linda over the last decade. Initially, I saw them up close when Cougar was a cub and in his early adulthood. This was a time that was very exciting for me professionally as well as for the three of them. It was a period of novelty and discovery for David and Linda as Cougar's owners, as well as for me as his doctor. Later, I saw them only from afar, after they moved to Florida.
>
> Cougar was my first exotic feline patient. He was unique because I have been able to see him go from a cub of eight pounds to an adult western cougar. He was already the size of most house cats when I first saw him as a cub.
>
> I saw David and Linda take Cougar through his first major illness after they returned from the Florida Keys. I saw the concern that David and Linda had for him—a concern every bit as deep as parents would have for their child. The problem we faced in treating Cougar for his illness was getting him to allow a blood sample necessary to figure out what to treat and how to treat it. We drew blood successfully only because David took his entire hand and put it into Cougar's mouth, between Cougar's two-inch canine teeth, while I took blood from his rear leg. There were three of us working with the rear leg. Two were holding it still. I was drawing blood. We were all nervous, to say the least. If X rays or an ultrasound had been necessary, it would have required that Cougar be anesthetized. He was the first severely ill big cat that I had treated. Diag-

nosing and treating Cougar without anesthesia taught me that I probably would never be able to do that with a large cat again unless it was David and Cougar.

The experience David has had with Cougar is certainly unique and has led to unusual experiences and great insight about big-cat behavior, both in the wild and in close relationships with people. As an individual, I do not believe in coincidences. In other words, I believe David's relationship with Cougar was meant to be. I also believe Linda's relationship with David was meant to be. He is a true blessing for Cougar. She is a blessing for both. Few women in this day and age would enjoy the experiences she has had with Cougar and David. The depth of David and Linda's relationship is also a blessing. I admire both of them, professionally and personally, and wish all three of them the very best. They deserve it.

After several days, Cougar began bounding around the house like a playful kitten. When he batted a hanging ivy plant and knocked a ficus tree over, I just smiled. We never found out what the problem was. What was interesting, though, was that the baby boy of the people we had been visiting in the Keys became sick with the same symptoms, and the sickness lasted the same three days.

COUGAR'S NEXT MEDICAL dilemma was more an injury than a sickness. It all started with my wanting him to have fun. But for a big cat having fun can be precarious. What could he enjoy that wouldn't be ingested or batted through the window or wall? Cats tend to find their own playthings—sometimes with fatal results, as when they play with string or electric cords. And a discarded grocery bag on the kitchen floor for Cougar was a tad small. So an ad appearing in a pet catalog caught my eye. The following ad appears even today.

THE ALMOST INDESTRUCTIBLE BALL

The Almost Indestructible Dog Ball is a 10" diameter, high-impact, polyethylene ball. Designed for "hard chewers," it won't chip, break, tear, or pop. We used to say it was totally indestructible, but a customer gave one to a lion.

So now, we say almost indestructible, just in case one of you knows an elephant!

Needless to say Cougar was the lion. The ball did seem like a fun toy, being too big to swallow and too light to go through the wall. Cougar was a hundred-pound, year-old teething toddler when I ordered the "indestructible" ball mentioned above. A package was sitting on my doorstep a week later. After Cougar ripped through the box, this shiny, slippery, red meteor streaked through the house. Not only did Cougar bat this featherweight bowling ball with no finger or thumb holes, but he squeezed it like a watermelon seed, launching it like a comet into the cosmos. Then he'd grasp it with his chest and arms and hold it with a vicelike grip, kicking it with his back feet and gouging it with his canines. It wasn't long before this shiny plastic ball had grooves gouged into its surface, which widened and deepened. It was obvious that it was just a matter of time before he'd penetrate the ball itself.

I notified the supplier and they sent me a replacement. While I waited, Cougar was forcing his teeth deeper and deeper into the first ball, until one day I heard a snap. Time stopped. Nothing is more important to me than Cougar's welfare. But as careful as I had been, the bottom quarter inch of his upper left canine was gone.

Norman and his son Kevin were my dentists. I had seen them several months previously for a checkup and Cougar had ridden along. I parked on the grass under a tree just outside their office window where I would be seated, and left him in the car. After sitting down, I casually mentioned that it'd be nice if I could bring Cougar inside. And to my delight the answer was yes. So Cougar ended up sitting on the floor next to me. Cougar watched Norman intently. "I'll be especially careful," Norman assured Cougar.

Norman was both a good dentist and interested in Cougar, so after Cougar's dental mishap we walked into his office, to the astonishment of a full waiting room. Everyone listened as I explained my dilemma to the receptionist, or should I say Cougar's. She said to have a seat. I sat on the floor and Cougar flipped upside down, spread-eagled on the carpet next to me. It wasn't long before Norman was at our side. "Hello, Cougar. I hear we've got a problem. Let's have a look."

In the middle of the waiting room, Norman adjusted the glasses sitting on the tip of his nose and bent down. I pushed Cougar's lip and whiskers out of the way. Norman grabbed his tooth. Cougar just looked at him. "Can you tilt your head back a little?" And to the astonishment of the crowd, Cougar did just that. "Hmm, that's got to hurt. See that red spot?" I nodded yes.

"That's pulp. It means that bacteria in his mouth can travel straight to his brain."

"What should we do?" I asked.

"I'd try the zoo."

The nurse, observing from the reception window, broke in. "Bruce Willis is a professor at the Indiana University School of Dentistry. He is also the zoo's dentist and nationally renowned for working on big cats." Gosh, how fortunate, I thought, right here in Indianapolis. I thanked Norman and his nurse, bid farewell to the patients in the waiting room—all of whom had completely forgotten their dental problems—and drove home.

I started by calling the Indianapolis Zoo and was essentially told to get lost—no empathy, no trying to help, no suggestions, and no directions. I'm sure their stance was, "Here's another exotic animal owner in over his head." Next I looked up Bruce's number and called. He was a breath of fresh air when I needed it. "Sure, bring him over so I can take a look."

I drove Cougar downtown to the dental school at the agreed-upon time, walked to a park bench just outside the main entrance, and waited. It wasn't long before a dark-haired man with a beard and blue eyes, clad in a three-quarter-length lab coat, was walking our way.

"Hello," I said, and after recognizing Bruce's name printed on his white coat joked, "How'd you know it was us?"

He looked around, playing as if he was looking for me, and answered, "Lucky guess."

I immediately liked Bruce's soft-spoken manner. He told me that Cougar's canine was still growing. The root canal was as big as a pencil, but after maturing it would reduce in size to a

pencil lead. A root canal procedure would kill the tooth, preventing further development, so a pulp cap was indicated, allowing the tooth to mature.

That afternoon I was on the phone with the Purdue University
School of Veterinary Medicine. They respected Bruce and agreed
that he could perform the procedure in their operating room and
they would provide the anesthesiologist and team. I was instructed to give Cougar a tranquilizer for the forty-five-minute
drive and was told he would then be anesthetized in the parking
lot and carted to the operating room. Tranquilization? Parking
lot? They obviously didn't know Cougar, or me for that matter.

Five days later, 1:30 P.M. on Tuesday, Cougar and I arrived.
Several television stations were there. At first I just wanted to be
left alone, but in retrospect, they were a welcome diversion. Then
a stocky man flanked by two female assistants walked up to the car.

"Hi, I'm Bob. I'll be your anesthesiologist."

His introduction made me feel comfortable. He didn't introduce himself as Dr. So-and-so, but as Bob. This unpretentiousness
was settling and he had an infectious smile. I rolled the window
down and he scratched Cougar behind the ear as he talked.

It wasn't long before he blurted out, "Maybe you could just
walk him in?"

And just as if the idea was new to me I responded, "That's a
great idea."

"Are we ready?" I asked.

"We are," Bob said, nodding to his assistants for agreement.

I opened the back door, but Cougar wasn't his natural self.
There were horses in a paddock and a dog on a leash not far
away. Normally, he would investigate both, intently staring and

sniffing, but not today. I wondered if my worry had an effect, as I slipped on his leash, whispering that everything would be all right. He stepped down ever so slowly.

I normally walk Cougar on grass rather than a sidewalk, thinking it had to feel better on his pads, but today I kept him on concrete, because the grass was covered with the feces of past patients. Then my thoughts ran wild. Was I doing the right thing? Norman did say that bacteria could get to his brain. Everything will be all right, I thought, trying to calm myself. But it sure didn't feel right.

The walkway led to a side entrance where a young man in a lab coat held the door. He smiled and I nodded. He directed us to proceed down to the basement. I smiled. The stairs were lined with hospital personnel and a television camera blinded me as we stepped down. At the bottom, a newsperson asked if I could go back up the stairs and come down again. My mind was on Cougar and getting him better—not making better pictures. I just shook my head and continued walking straight ahead. I was sick with worry.

I followed a technician down a concrete block hallway painted a pale green and turned left into a small room lined with cages—no blankets or toys, just bars. How many people were instructed to leave their trusted four-legged family member and return days later? Would they do the same with their two-legged progeny? Why are we still under the illusion that cats and dogs don't need our support? Unbelievably, it wasn't very long ago when the medical profession believed that animals didn't experience physical pain and actually operated on them without anesthesia. Now, how long will it be before they realize animals experience emotional pain? Rows upon rows of empty eyes watched us as we passed. How much loneliness does it take to create apathy when a mountain lion walks by?

We then entered a huge operating theater. It was cold. The minutest sound reverberated off stainless steal cabinets, a concrete ceiling, and a linoleum floor. It was so clean it hurt. The smell of disinfectant permeated the air. There were seven individual operating stations, with their own sinks, oxygen cylinders, and overhead fluorescent lights casting a blue-white light sharp enough to slash.

I walked over and joined Bruce as he stood back and admired an unrolled cloth case displaying his instruments.

"Hello," he said. "I made all these by hand. They're ten times larger than human instruments."

Bob walked up, confirmed Cougar's weight, and computed the anesthetic dosage. "We'll inject Cougar with ketamine/xylazine and then intubate him with isoflurane and oxygen. After Bruce is done, we unhook Cougar and in five minutes he jumps off the table and walks to the car. But this shot stings. We'll have to tie him to an operating table." He grabbed the massive support. "This has held a horse—it should do. Wrap his leash around it several times and, please, no slack!"

"That won't be necessary," I said, choking back emotion. "Are we ready?"

Everyone nodded.

I cradled Cougar's head and put my hand in his mouth. "It's like sucking his thumb," I whispered. The time had come. I laid my face next to his whiskers and whispered, "I'll be right here . . . you are my bestest kitty." I nodded that we were ready. Somewhat in awe, Bob positioned himself. Cougar watched as Bob grabbed a roll of muscle from his thigh and flicked his wrist like throwing a dart. The two-and-a-half-inch needle disappeared into fur and the plunger pressed home.

Cougar flinched, softly mouthing my hand with a soft, guttural complaint. "It's okay," I whispered, desperately wishing it were so. I felt his head wobble, then go limp, and watched his third eyelid, like a curtain, ever so slowly glide across his eye.

"We need some help here," Bob yelled.

I cradled Cougar's head, neck, and shoulders, Bob scooped under his midsection, and an assistant brought up the rear. Lifting in unison, we placed Cougar on the operating table. Bob immediately got to work, feeding a long plastic tube into his mouth, down his throat, and into his windpipe. After connecting flexible hoses, he set the isoflurane/oxygen mixture to 5 percent. Assistants then shaved the inside of Cougar's right arm and leg for intravenous saline. A vital signs monitor, a machine with small, red LED lights—glimmering numbers indicating pulse, blood pressure, temperature, and respiration—kept everyone apprised of how Cougar was doing. All this for a simple pulp cap. Welcome to the world of animal medicine, where little problems became big ones.

Cougar was intubated, IV'd, and monitored, and the numbers were right. Bruce called for X rays to be taken; and after they were developed he looked at the ghostly images, which confirmed what we already knew. Then that noise we all dread—the squeal of the dentist's drill. But the pain wasn't the patient's, it was mine.

Bruce, using a disc, made rough edges smooth. Then, with a

drill, he cleaned out exposed pulp to a depth of one or two centimeters and, with forceps, took a small piece of cotton soaked with calcium hydroxide and swabbed the pulp cavity. A tooth-colored glass ionomer was prepared, packed, and formed into a cap. Then a special purple light was placed in Cougar's mouth for five minutes, bonding the cap to his tooth. There . . . he was done. All the preparation, the anesthesia, the X rays, the assistants, the doctors, and the film crews, all to cap a tooth. But we weren't out of the woods yet.

"Should Cougar chew on one side?" I asked, trying to make light of the moment.

"Not necessary," Bruce said with a chuckle.

Cougar hadn't moved during the entire procedure and Bob had, step-by-step, reduced the isoflurane from 5 percent to 0.75 percent. Now it was time to disconnect Cougar from those cylinders, allowing him to breathe air through the intubation tube. This tube's purpose now was just to keep the passageway to his lungs clear until he woke up.

I watched the clock on the wall, not unlike the one back in grade school. Cougar didn't move. I remembered Bob's prognosis, five minutes until he would jump off the table and walk to the car.

It was now three times that.

Bob took Cougar's lower jaw and moved it in a chewing fashion, then side to side. No reaction. He was puzzled. I didn't like puzzled.

Cougar's IV and monitor were removed, but he was still unconscious, so his intubation tube remained down his throat. Bob then rolled a cart next to the operating table.

"Help me roll Cougar on the cart."

With several assistants stabilizing both ends, I grabbed his back legs and Bob grabbed his collar and front legs, and together we scooted Cougar to the cart.

"Okay, let's take him to your car."

Everyone wanted to help, or give him a pat, but Cougar just lay there. The only sign of life was the slow, rhythmic roll of his side as he breathed. They all helped push the cart, squeezing through the operating room door, down the hallway, around the corner, up the ramp, and out the door. Like ants carrying a bug, they all moved together without a sound.

Bob broke the hush. "We'll wait here while you get your car."

I nodded and ran as fast as I could, not because Cougar needed a ride, but because I didn't want to leave him. I quickly unlocked the Grand Cherokee, started the engine, and drove back. There he was, a seemingly lifeless form, lying on the cart surrounded by well-wishers. I lowered the back window and Bob opened the tailgate. He crawled in on all fours, turned around, and ordered the group to push the cart closer.

Grabbing two furry handles, Bob pulled while I pushed, and together we slid Cougar into the back of the car. Bob then sat cross-legged and placed Cougar's head in his lap. "Come on, fellah," he said, shaking Cougar's bottom jaw. Cougar made a feeble response. "That-a-boy, fight me." He shook Cougar's jaw again, and this time Cougar fought back a little harder. "That's it." This continued for forty-five minutes. Finally Bob removed the intubation tube and, with much difficulty, scooted his stiff body from the back of the car. He stood for a moment, rubbing his arms and legs. "I wouldn't advise returning until Cougar can at least support his head," he said. I thanked him. Then everyone was gone.

It was silent: no more television cameras, doctors, medical assistants, or staff. For the next hour, it was just Cougar and me, face to face. Then, finally, Cougar with a wobbly head was ready and we departed.

It was dark when we pulled out of the parking lot. After reaching the highway, I engaged the cruise control, arched my back over the top of the seat, tilted the rearview mirror down, and extended my free hand back into the dark space where Cougar was recovering. He bumped the back of my hand with his dry nose. I felt better. We were together. And that's the way I remained until several blocks from home.

It must have been a familiar smell. Cougar struggled forward and, with his nose, pushed all the way up to my arm to my shoulder, giving me chills. Then he heaved with all his might, using his chin and neck to lift his body until he could feebly stand. With his muzzle next to my ear he tried to chirp, but nothing came out. So with his tongue he touched my cheek. I sighed. He would be all right. It was I who would never be the same.

THAT CAP REMAINED in place for six years, but in December 1997 it cracked and started breaking away. We had moved to Florida, so I sought help from the College of Veterinary Medicine at the University of Florida in Gainesville. To say things were different there is an understatement. Yes, I'm sure they treated animals' physical ailments well but their bedside manner, their concern for the animals' psychological health, was a different story.

You see, I believe animals act the way they are treated. When creatures, human or otherwise, lash out, there is a reason. And to label those actions as wild is a cop-out, taking no thought. Life isn't that simple. Animals act a certain way either because of having to survive or because of being treated that way. Humans are no different. We confine several big cats who are solitary by nature in public cages and throw in raw meat when they're hungry. How would house cats behave in the same situation? How about hungry human prisoners?

And on the other side of the equation, how would big cats behave after being treated like house cats? In Cougar's case, trust me, the answer is better. But I don't mean to imply that big cats make good pets, for it's imperative, given their strength, that you be in tune with them—every second.

So how should one treat a cat? First, relate; then use the golden rule. I believe abandoning an animal, allowing him or her to go through a traumatic situation alone, is abusive. Examples include abandoning pets during disasters, as well as the widely accepted practice of shipping animals in crates. And, closer to the point, dropping pets off at the vet. Since when would you drop your child off at the hospital and return when he or she was ready to come home? Did I hear someone say that children aren't animals? How about human animals? Does that mean other animals can't experience emotion? Oh, did I hear someone answer that animals don't feel emotion as deeply as we? Sounds like human bias again.

The fact of the matter is that abandonment hurts. Did you ever consider that some veterinarians want you out of their hair? Do animals understand the necessity for their medical procedure? Of course not! Neither do children; that's why it's so important to be there for them. But both children and animals understand being abandoned. And just because felines have the most self-centered personalities on this planet doesn't mean they shun companionship during hardship. From their standpoint, it hurt and you weren't there. Ever wonder why cats hide when their carrier is brought out? If stressful situations were handled differently, they'd willingly leap for it.

It's important to look at the world through the eyes of the animal or person you are trying to help. When you use your own eyes, you are only helping yourself. Concerning medical matters, I believe we must consider physical and psychological health simultaneously. In other words, relate to them and then treat them as you would want to be treated. After all, if our brains are what makes us different from animals, let's try using them.

So it's back to a case in point. Avery Bennett was in charge of Small Animal Clinical Sciences at the University of Florida's College of Veterinary Medicine and Dr. Helmick was the doctor in charge when we arrived. I had planned that Cougar would demonstrate, as at Purdue, that he shouldn't be lumped together with all those mistreated cats. I was hoping that the generalities, the sensational big-cat mentality, and the wild-cat labels didn't prevail here. But I was sadly mistaken.

We arrived at the Gainesville Small Animal Clinic at eight in the morning to have Cougar's tooth fixed. Everyone watched and all were visibly impressed by his demeanor, but nothing

changed. I was instructed to leave Cougar and go sit in the waiting room. A half hour later a sweet technician walked up with
bitter news. They had shot Cougar with an anesthetic dart. Anesthetic darts are dangerous and should be used only when a
safer means of anesthesia cannot be utilized. She promised to
return and let me know how he was doing.

An hour or so later, a man in scrubs walked up, introduced
himself as doctor So-and-so, and explained that Cougar's tooth
had never fully matured. It was "paper thin" and he was apprehensive about applying another cap, fearing he'd break the
tooth in the process. He highly recommended extraction. I
said absolutely not. After all, Cougar had done well with that
tooth for six years and I'd do my best to keep it that way for
another six, and another, and another. Doctor So-and-so
seemed disappointed: he didn't get to pull the canine tooth
from a mountain lion every day, if he ever had before. He
turned around grudgingly and walked away. An hour later, the
same sweet technician informed me that Cougar was in recovery. I followed her back.

There he was, on his side, tongue hanging out, in an enclosure looking more like a shower stall, with bars in place of
a curtain and a tile floor allowing God knows what all to be
hosed down the drain. I lay down next to him and someone
shut the door behind me, informing me that animals were
"wild" when they came out of anesthesia. I thought to myself,
You would be, too, after being shot with a dart, waking up in
a strange place surrounded by strangers, and experiencing
unexplained pains. Maybe humans act better because they understand what's going on. All the more reason why we need to

be with animals during their uncertainty. So Cougar, my pants, and my shirt all mopped the floor. I knew his head would be unsteady, so asked for a towel and rolled it into a pillow. It seemed strange that no longer than an hour ago doctor So-and-so had told me he feared cracking Cougar's tooth with his delicate instruments and now Cougar was placed in a unpad-ded cage, when his head and body would be crashing about during recovery. And it took much longer than expected for Cougar to recover. But at Purdue, the doctor had been right there.

Here it was different. There was no doctor, as a matter of fact; no one was there. When Cougar staggered and lurched, it was difficult, holding his collar, to prevent him from banging into the walls. For two and a half hours we bumped and stum-bled together. Finally he was steady enough to walk to the car. I yelled, but no one was there. I stuck my hand through the bars and reached around for the latch. It was locked. Oh great, I thought.

Don't get me wrong; I desperately wanted to be with Cougar as he recovered. And they bent their rules in allowing me to be with him. But where was everybody? It seemed a little strange that they would dart Cougar, throw him into an unpadded re-covery cell, allow me to join him, lock the door, and leave. The reason for all their restrictions was that certain animals were considered wild. Then what about my safety? And much more important, what if Cougar needed help? An hour later, a tech-nician strolled by and I asked him to unlock the door.

After returning home, I wrote to Avery regarding his facility's lack of logic. The following was his reply:

Mr. Raber,

I am writing in response to your letter dated 1-26-98. I have reviewed "Cougar's" medical record and spoken with the staff involved during his visit here in December of 1996 [*sic;* he meant to write 1997]. It appears that there are some significant discrepancies. In themselves, they may seem insignificant but it concerns me that I may not be able to expect an honest assessment from you in the future.

You indicate in your letter that Cougar was darted, yet it appears from our records that he was hand injected while in a squeeze cage. The staff indicated that you actually led him into the squeeze. . . .

Finally, the staff has told me that, though you were allowed to be with your cat during recovery, at no point were you "locked with him as he recovered while no one was around." These issues cause serious concern in me because your perception is so vastly different from that of my staff, which I respect implicitly, often with my life. . . .

Sincerely,
R. Avery Bennett, D.V.M., M.S., Diplomate A.C.V.S.
Assistant Professor, Zoo and Wildlife Medicine

All animals rely on trust. I appreciate Dr. Bennett allowing me to use his letter demonstrating human animals are no different. I hope his practice is in better hands now.

I NOW KNEW that Cougar's left canine was undeveloped. What could he chew on that would clean his teeth, but not fracture his canine? Rawhide bones seemed like a good idea, but they were too hard. So I soaked them in water until they became pliable, and he consumed one large bone a day. In the process, I learned that not all rawhide bones are created equal. Some are just scraps rolled up with a wrapper like a cigar. I also discovered that after soaking, the U.S. hides didn't smell like garbage in the sun, but the foreign ones, rampant with bacteria, did.

But after a year of *bone*-fide enjoyment, Cougar started having problems. His urine became discolored with blood, which I thought was a sign of infection, so I treated him with antibiotics. The bleeding stopped. Several months later, he started passing blood in his urine again. Something wasn't right.

Neil Shaw, Cougar's temporary veterinary specialist at the time, coordinated X rays. David Murphy, the chief veterinarian for the Lowry Park Zoo in Tampa, performed the anesthesia. Anesthesia scares me, always will. Zoo cats for David were an everyday occurrence, so working with Cougar was like a walk in the park. By the way, Avery referred to a "squeeze" in his letter; that is a cage out of an old horror movie. It restrains an animal when the sides squeeze together. A cat will object violently, bashing his head into the bars, breaking teeth in the process. With David there is knowledgeable experience. I just walk Cougar past him; he swings a syringe and pushes the plunger in one continuous motion. If you blink, you miss it. Cougar jumps in a knee-jerk reaction and then walks to a comfortable place to snooze. When he gets wobbly in five or six minutes, I walk him to the X-ray room and wait until he's completely out. There's nothing terrifying, nothing upsetting, and there's no risk of harming him with a dart; just a kind, humane, and safe treatment. And I'm right there when he wakes up.

The X rays revealed that Cougar's kidneys were packed with calcium oxalate stones and his kidney function was being adversely affected. The normal procedure to eliminate this problem is very intrusive. The kidneys are surgically exposed, sliced in half, opened up, and the stones picked out. Richard Funk, Cougar's veterinarian of record since we moved to Florida, had read about a technique called lithotripsy and suggested checking into it as an alternative. With lithotripsy, the patient is either partially submerged in a tub of water or, in the portable unit, lies on a plate of vegetable oil. An ultrasound machine is aimed, the stones are pounded into fragments from outside the body, and the resulting debris is passed in the urine. This is technology developed for humans. People go through this procedure every day with just a light tranquilizer. But it's a little difficult telling Cougar to hold that position for a half hour or so.

Michael Binder, board certified in urology, sometimes calls an eighteen-wheeler an operating room. This portable lithotripsy unit was driven to Lowry Park Zoo and parked outside David's office. Cougar arrived, met Michael's wife, Amy, and children, and all the zoo personnel. When he strolled past David, there was a little sting. Cougar turned to look at David with a not-you-again expression, and he was off to slumberland.

As before, he was intubated, IV'd, and attached to a vital signs monitor. His belly was shaved and he was placed tummy down on a plate with a quarter-inch of vegetable oil. The stones were located by a fluoroscope. Then ultrasound waves issued from what looked like an automobile spark plug screwed into a dish-like focusing device. The patient's pulse is used to synchronize this firing sequence, and the machine fires between heartbeats so as not to throw the heart into arrythmia. Zap . . . zap . . . zap . . . The machine fires between the beats of the patient's heart.

In the process, I discovered that cats' kidneys float around; so during the procedure, Michael would check to see if the crosshairs were still on the stones. After the procedure the stones, on X ray, looked less dense, changed from a bright white to more of a gray. Good riddance!

BUT I WANTED to know why Cougar had stones in the first place. The more I dug into the problem, the more I discovered how little is known. One thing was certain: I was going to test Cougar's urine every time he voided. In so doing, I immediately knew what was going on regarding leukocytes, nitrate, urobilinogen, protein, pH, blood, specific gravity, ketones, bilirubin, and glucose. If Cougar had the hiccups, I wanted to know. I'd recommend every concerned animal lover do the same for his or her animals at least once a week.

The test strips indicate the presence of red blood cells on an ascending scale: negative, trace, $+$, $++$, and $+++$. Immediately after the procedure Cougar passed a lot of red blood cells, but after a week his urine was completely free of them—though, occasionally, he'd register a trace and then return to normal. Several months later, however, he grabbed a section of carpet in his teeth and bit down hard. I scolded him, but he did it again. He just wasn't acting normally. Then when we were out of town on a trip he registered $+++$ and it stayed that way for two weeks. Something wasn't right.

After returning home we went back for more X rays and discovered debris lodged in his ureter, the tube leading from the right kidney to the urinary bladder. I am told that passing stones is excruciatingly painful for humans and that cats don't seem to mind. Hogwash. Animals don't show pain like we do, but it hurts. Cats aren't yelling and screaming, but believe me, Cougar was not comfortable. He bit down hard on the carpet for several reasons. One, it's like human patients being given something to bite down on in lieu of anesthesia. And two, getting my attention, even by making me angry, meant I would help.

All I had were questions. What caused the stones? And how much of a blockage did he have? Neil wanted to take a wait-and-see approach, but I wasn't comfortable with that. If Cougar was still producing stones, it would be only a matter of time before one would pass down his ureter and lodge against the mass already there, and we'd have total blockage. When that happens there is no place for the urine to go, pressure builds, and the kidney dies. Humans and cats can comfortably survive on one healthy kidney. But Cougar's kidneys had been compromised; he needed both. I wasn't going to play "wait and see."

Neil suggested we get a second opinion. Dennis Chew from the Ohio State University Veterinary Hospital is known for treating urinary tract problems in animals. He brought in Bruce Woodworth, a medical doctor from Ohio Urology, Inc., who possessed the knowledge needed, because feline bladder disease is similar to a condition afflicting women. The game plan was to scope Cougar, threading a catheter up past the urinary bladder to the blockage, and have a look. The blockage could be examined, then blasted away or moved down into the urinary bladder, and out.

On June 22, 1999, Cougar Raber showed up at Ohio Kidney

Stone Center in Columbus and walked in just as he if he were human. Bruce immediately felt that scoping, though interesting, was intrusive. Further, he knew what the problem was and how to fix it: lithotripsy. Cougar's first lithotripsy procedure had been done with a portable unit—high and dry, with just a little oil. The equipment in Columbus utilized a tub of water, presenting a unique problem: immersing a fully anesthetized, two-hundred-pound cat in the water, positioning him, and keeping him warm. Further, the trapeze that would be used to lower Cougar into the water was designed for humans. When Cougar, under general anesthesia, was lowered into the water, his fully relaxed body slouched through every nook and cranny of the trapeze. It took three of us to push these folds back where they belonged so as to avoid pressure points. Two and a half hours later, he still wasn't positioned correctly. Bruce commented afterwards: "I was impressed with the flexibility of his torso and in particular his spine. Obviously, large cats were designed to have that flexibility for speed, agility, and climbing."

There was another problem. Bruce wrote later, "things were going smoothly until Cougar's feces in his terminal colon got in the way and prevented us from being able to see the stone from the one angle." I did say Cougar was never hungry.

Finally, Cougar's ureteral blockage was under the crosshairs. But the lithotripsy machine didn't have his pulse. Remember, the ultrasound waves are fired between heartbeats. Cougar's skin was much thicker than human skin and the leads weren't picking up his pulse. Makeshift leads with pins were hastily constructed and stuck under his skin, but still no pulse could be monitored.

Bruce said that because the ureteral mass was so far away from the heart, he was going into manual mode, allowing the machine to zap away without being in sync with Cougar's resting heart—cardiac arrythmia shouldn't be a problem. I didn't just say no, I said hell no. I wasn't going to have a seemingly small problem become a much bigger one. I thought for a moment, then suggested, "Why don't you move the leads closer to Cougar's heart?"

They all looked at each other with a shrug—why not? A tech shaved two new areas directly over his heart and the leads were stuck in place. We had a pulse!

Video cameras and newspaper reporters were there. I was informed that the *Columbus Dispatch* reporter, ErinMarie, was complaining that I had not granted her an interview and she was tired of waiting. These folks just don't get it. I'm there for Cougar, not them.

But ErinMarie was persistent. She finally corralled Linda for an interview that resulted in a front-page story stating that Linda owned Cougar. Well, I suppose it's all a matter of perspective, but no one "owns" Cougar. And ErinMarie wasn't finished.

X rays disclosed that not only did Cougar have a blockage, but stones had reformed in both kidneys. So after the ureteral mass was blasted, Bruce stared at the fluoroscope, guiding the crosshairs to the left kidney. ErinMarie tapped him on the shoulder.

Cougar's welfare was indeed extremely important to Bruce, but his technicians could handle the procedure for a minute or two without him. He and ErinMarie walked a short distance away from the screen for an interview while the technicians continued aiming the machine. But I wanted Bruce. I watched as the crosshairs were maneuvered over a nondescript radiograph roadmap of Cougar's insides, and listened to Bruce answering ErinMarie's questions. Finally I couldn't take it any longer. I took several steps toward ErinMarie and said as firmly as I dared, "Will you please excuse the doctor!"

After four hours and fifteen minutes we were done and Cougar was taken off isoflurane. This time the problem wasn't too much anesthetic, but too much time under anesthesia. The shackles of a drugged nap of four-plus hours kept Cougar pinned to the mat. And after an hour of his being unable to get up, a stretcher was summoned. As we tried to scoot him onto the stretcher, he decided otherwise. Wobbly, but under his own power, he stumbled to the car.

I WAS THANKFUL that Cougar could benefit from human technology that allowed a nonintrusive way of getting rid of stones, but I didn't want this to be an annual affair. I wanted to know what was causing these stones.

First, I checked genetics: What about his mother and father? I discovered that his mother had died at the age of seven (Cougar's age when I discovered he had a kidney stone problem) from "blood disease"—an uneducated catchall phrase covering any unknown ailment. Her symptoms were exactly the same as kidney failure. And how about Cougar's father? He was sold, and sold, and sold again. A life so seemingly insignificant that records weren't even kept. Such is the fate of exotic animals. In the wild, cougars are shot from trees or hit by cars. And in captivity they are sold repeatedly until they die. Seems unfair, but it's human bias again. I mean it's illegal to shoot a human being without cause, and hitting a person with a car is called manslaughter. And slavery is not only unlawful, but morally wrong. So what gives? I know, I know, they're just animals. We can kill them, but they can't return the favor.

So it appears that Cougar inherited this problem. I discovered that his urinary pH lingered around 5.9, an acidity increasing the possibility that calcium oxalate stones would form. But what was triggering this formation? Each and every time a sample of his blood was sent to the lab, the results were absolutely normal.

Since I had been checking Cougar's urine at least three times a day for several years, I noticed a trend. He would always pass a major amount of red blood cells after consuming rawhide bones. I mentioned this to all the doctors involved, but no one believed that rawhide could cause kidney stones. So, because Cougar so dearly loved eating rawhide, I allowed him to continue chomping away. His first bout with lithotripsy occurred when he was seven and a half—after a year of eating rawhide bones. His second bout with lithotripsy was a year later—after continuing to eat rawhide bones. Granted, he was eating a lot of rawhide, one medium-size bone a day, but that didn't sound unnatural given that he was a carnivore.

So Cougar's problem continued. And when he has a problem, I have a problem. Frequently we just know enough to get ourselves into trouble, but I wasn't about to follow the prevailing educated guesses, which reminded me of my experience with diabetes. Twenty years ago, after being diagnosed with diabetes,

I was told that sugar kills and that I should increase my intake of fat. So for about a year I rationalized that cheesecake was good for me—until I had had enough. After all, we are what we eat. It made sense to eat healthy, exercise, and control my high blood sugar with insulin. Seems simple now, but this approach has kept my blood sugar normal, and I'm free of diabetic complications. Actually, I'm healthier now than I would have been if I wasn't afflicted. I want the same for Cougar.

I would attack Cougar's problem the same way. I would put him on the healthiest diet available. I'd say *bunk* to those suggesting I reduce his calcium intake. When your body wants to build a calcium stone it will find the material somehow. If not through diet, it will break down bones and teeth, so it made no sense to cut back on Cougar's dietary intake of calcium, starving his body of an essential mineral. And I wasn't cutting back on protein, because cats are carnivores. Their entire being depends on eating meat.

The diabetic diet has become the best example of what all people should eat. Cougar's diet will be the same regarding all cats, big and small. And as I depend on insulin, he would require potassium citrate.

After a year of applying these principles, it was time to take Cougar in for more X rays and see if I was right. Radiographs confirmed that there were no new stones and whatever calcium oxalate debris remained was melting away like a spring snow. Helping matters was that he wanted to get better because he was happy, knowing I was there.

9

FOOD FOR THOUGHT

"CULTURE, CUSTOMERS, PRODUCTS, people" . . . *and Cougar*. I add Cougar to the Iams motto because he's as important as all the rest to me. And speaking of important, diet is, too—for all of us. We are, after all, what we eat, so providing the best nutrition for Cougar is my way of ensuring he's the best he can be.

When Cougar was three months old, in 1991, I started feeding him what was considered the top zoo food for felines. It was based on the technology of the sixties and came in fourteen-ounce cans. He was now seven. A lot had been learned about nutrition since then and I wanted it.

After nosing around among the world's top animal nutritionists, I discovered Marcie Strieker (to become Campion a year later), manager of regulatory affairs for research and development at the Iams Company. I didn't expect what I found. Yes, Marcie was knowledgeable, gracious, and friendly. And yes, I was impressed with the product. But it was much more: the corporate culture and the people like Marcie spun me around.

First was the product. Cougar started eating Eukanuba, named after a Hoagy Carmichael expression meaning ooh-la-la. For Hoagy it meant the best-looking woman; for pet lovers it means the best you can do for your cat or dog. Cougar thrived on it. He was always considered a "10" by zoo standards, but after eating "Euk" he glowed in the dark. So Marcie called Jeff

Warmouth, the Eukanuba cat food assistant brand manager at the time, and explained that this particular, two-hundred-pound cat prospered on their product. Jeff was working on a big cat/little cat promotional theme at the time, so he telephoned me. After several conversations, both he and Lara Strazdin, manager of their communications department, flew to Tampa to see for themselves.

I suggested that we meet at Landry's, a local waterfront restaurant. Landry's, like TGI Fridays, Bennigan's Key West Grill, and other eateries in the Tampa/St. Petersburg/Clearwater area, all extend an invitation for Cougar to come and munch lunch. After Jeff and Lara landed and rented a car, they made their way to our meeting place, walking past palm trees and palmettoes toward the front door. The movie theater marquee high over their heads read: "Welcome Cougar and the Iams Company."

Jeff has light brown hair and a six-foot-one, athletic build. He played basketball back in school, but now scoring points means achieving a greater market share. Lara has long reddish-brown hair with an appealing crook in her smile. They approached the hostess and announced, "We're here to see Cougar."

"Oh yes, follow me," was the answer.

Landry's sits on Tampa Bay with a deck overlooking calm, shallow waters. Jet Skis and flat-bottom crab boats crisscross the surface. Above, commercial airliners pass in front of a Tampa skyline, descending to the airport. When Cougar visits, there is an out-of-the-way table at one end of the deck; it is a perfect place for the mannerly feline to have a snack. But today he didn't care to remain out in the sun, and his tummy was full, since he had already eaten, so I pulled the car around on the grass and parked under a palm tree, allowing him to hang out and keep me in sight. That's where he was when Jeff and Lara joined Linda and me.

After initial pleasantries, Jeff asked, "Can Cougar do any tricks?" I answered no. The "trick" is his comfort. I know Cougar and he knows me and our trust is unwavering. Cougar, with no instruction, no practice, no food for enticement, can accomplish much more than trained cats. He does it for me. Relationships are stronger than food—love is stronger than hunger.

But relationships take time. There's no substitute for hours and hours of positive time. What do you believe is the effect on the behavior of POWs confined behind bars? Are cats any different? Felinity is extraordinary. Mix it with positive time and you've got something special. Cats, just like us, behave the way they are treated regardless of their size. We have been taught that big cats behaviorally differ from small cats—wild versus domestic, ferocious versus tame, night versus day—which is the same as saying big strong people are more aggressive than weaker, smaller people, which, if the truth were known, is probably just the reverse.

By now all those having lunch were straining to see the big shadow in the car. Cougar had been here before. I whispered, "It's show time." Jeff, Lara, and Linda followed me down the steps to the car and as I approached Cougar, he chirped hello. "Do you want to come out and see everyone?" I asked. "Chirp" was his response. That's a yes, I said, smiling back at Jeff. Everyone on the deck crowded to the railing and those inside pushed up against the window as Cougar stepped down on freshly mowed grass and took center stage immediately in front of eight-foot-high mangroves at the water's edge. I pointed to his hip. "Sit please." Cougar sat down. "Now could you stand up for me?" Cougar stood and put his arm on my shoulder. Jeff whispered to Lara, "Right—he doesn't do any tricks."

After Cougar and I had spent fifteen minutes entertaining the lunch crowd, we all walked back to the car, where Jeff fed Cougar a Eukanuba cat food snack by hand. "Gosh," Jeff remarked, "he's so gentle." Cougar was on his way to becoming the spokescat for Eukanuba cat food, made by the Iams Company. There might be someone suggesting that I'm exploiting him, but nothing is farther from the truth. It reminds me of sitting on the flight deck of an aircraft carrier about to be catapulted off into the wild blue yonder in one of the highest-performance aircraft of the day—and getting paid for it. Working for the Iams Company is just like that. I'm encouraging others to feed their cats the same great food Cougar eats and in so doing I can spend more time with him.

The Iams Company is in the pet food business, but for the people it's much more. Walk through the main doors of their corporate headquarters in Dayton, Ohio, stroll through the lobby, and you are greeted with an operatic zing by Artie. Artie sang opera to put herself through college.

Curled up on the floor next to Artie is Kersee, the golden retriever. Kersee lies with her muzzle on the ground. Her eyes acknowledge everyone as they pass, but her tail only swishes for friends. Kersee is getting on in years, so you must excuse her for not getting up and thrusting her nose where she shouldn't.

Walk down the hall and you might see a partially opened file cabinet with a fuzzy feline face peering over the top, following your every move. Then there are plaster of paris dogs standing sentry by conference room doors. One of the dogs is now missing his muzzle: Cougar wiped the smirk off his face with one swipe.

This is creature country, a place for animal lovers and critters, famous and not. Several months after meeting Jeff and Lara, Cougar was at Iams. The television celebrity Jack Hanna was there, too. He looked at Cougar. Cougar looked at him and Jack announced that he would have to change the signs on the cougar display at the Columbus Zoo. Cougar looked different—half-again bigger, and his coat sparkled like diamonds. "What do you feed him?" he asked in astonishment. The answer, Eukanuba cat food. Jack responded in his Tennessean drawl, "Eukanuba! Gol dang."

Cats are carnivores. In nature, they eat whole animals commensurate to their size: mice for kitties and deer for big cats. Big cats don't normally prey on mice because they can quickly dart into places too tight for a big cat pursuer. House cats don't prey on deer because they can't capture them. But if catching prevalent numbers of mice were effortless for a big cat and Kitty could capture a deer, both cats would be healthy. What's nourishing for one is nourishing for the other, too.

As food for felines, mice and deer are nutritionally balanced. They're meat, muscle and organs, along with other stuff. The top two ingredients in Eukanuba are muscle and organs—animal protein. It doesn't take a rocket scientist to recognize that substituting plant for animal protein won't work. In a million years of feline evolution, I'll bet there hasn't been one cat who has dug up a soybean and eaten it. There's a reason. Sure, some cats eat veggies, but not as a staple diet. Okay, okay, enough. It's show time—the thrill of being eye to eye with a big cat, watching him eat, lick his paws, roll over, sit up, and play, just like Kitty back home.

There was no time to prepare for our first event, the Houston Cat Show, so Cougar, Linda, and I drove to Houston, Texas, and showed up at the George R. Brown Convention Center with only my gift of gabbing about Cougar. Show regulations didn't allow Cougar to be with the smaller kitties, which was just fine by me. The only place available was a room three floors up from the main show. A partition of bi-fold doors divided this big room into two smaller areas, each could accommodate 150 chairs. We had no idea how many attendees would travel three floors from the main event, and we wished to create a more intimate setting, so we closed the bi-fold partition.

At one end, the stage was positioned against a glass block wall, then stanchions, then chairs arranged in rows. At the appointed time, Cougar stepped down from his car, which was parked on a third-floor loading ramp, and walked through a freight door and down the long hall. He peeked around the door of our room to check it out, then, after the oohs subsided, I introduced him and took center stage in front of an audience of about thirty.

I began explaining what it was like to live with a two-hundred-pound cat and why I was against exotic-animal ownership. Word spread. Pretty soon, the entire room was packed and the bi-fold doors were opened. Before I knew it, 300 seats were occupied and people stood around the perimeter and along the back. Dale Barger, the Iams national event leader, commented later that if a speaker can hold a crowd's attention for fifteen minutes, that's good; an hour is exceptional. These people were glued to their seats for more than three hours and the line outside the door snaked down the hall to the escalator. Jeff gave me the cut signal, but I couldn't resist answering "just one more question." I stopped talking after three hours and forty-five minutes.

But the audience didn't leave. Some pressed forward, asking more questions. Finally, Jeff announced that Cougar needed a rest. Actually, Cougar had been resting the entire time. I fed him Eukanuba by hand, and his water bowl piled high with ice was at his side, Blankie and Nursey were under his arm, his tray was close if nature called, and if he wanted to stretch, he'd step off the stage, sniff around, then hop back as I explained what he was doing and why. But much of the time he just acted like a house cat and watched the audience.

Houston was fun. Though my presentation needed refining, it was spontaneous and from the heart. I had to learn to be succinct and answer questions more concisely, all without losing compassion and warmth. Have no doubt though, the impromptu sincerity and closeness of Houston will always be special.

Next was Boston—more refined, but still close. Cameras for the evening news filmed Cougar yawning and me talking. We weren't three floors away from the main show this time, but just on the other side of double doors. The primary sponsor was

Friskies, with their animal show, but it was Cougar who was on everyone's lips. Friskies demanded that Cougar's show be on the half hour; they would be on the hour. Sounded like a good plan, but it depended on me talking thirty minutes or less. Fat chance. The line for Cougar's next performance snaked around the coliseum, past the vacant Friskies show, and beyond. Friskies should have been happy having customers stand in line along their booth while waiting for Cougar's show, compliments of Eukanuba, but I don't think they were.

FEW WOULD ARGUE with the fact that Cougar was the main attraction wherever he went, but Jeff needed to sell upper management on the idea of Cougar being their spokescat, which wasn't as easy as reviewing Cougar's résumé, scheduling an interview, and seeing how he fielded questions. So how does one schedule an interview with a two-hundred-pound cat, given the hectic itineraries of top management? Coincidentally, Iams was having a national sales conference in Puerto Rico and all the top brass would be there. But I said I would not put Cougar in a cage and the airlines weren't hot on the idea of him sitting in a seat, first class or not. And there was no time for an island cruise. Aircraft charter was the only alternative. What was important to Iams was not the cost, but whatever made Cougar comfortable. The most economical bid was from a local Lear jet operator, so I sprang the passenger list: Linda, me, and Cougar. "That's a cute name for a cat," was his response. I answered, "It only seems natural . . . for a cougar." There was a pause long enough for me to swim to Puerto Rico. Then a shout: "Really!" He loved the idea. All he had to do was sell it to his crew of two. So at the appointed time, Cougar stepped up into the aircraft, lay on the couch, and looked out the window as we rolled along the taxiway, roared down the runway, lifted, and flew like a bird. His nose glued to the window, he looked down on seagulls and clouds. There was no doubt he knew he was flying. We were on our way to Puerto Rico, a self-governing commonwealth of the United States whose joint official languages are Spanish and English. Granted, this Caribbean island had laws similar to ours, but I was worried about possible language problems, and didn't want to find myself and Cougar confined in some distant dungeon, where no one was the least bit interested in my no-cages policy, for both of us.

I had applied for and received all my permits, but I wanted assurance that all would be well. By checking with the U.S. Department of Agriculture, Cougar's federal licensing authority, I discovered another Linda, a respected island veterinarian who was once a USDA inspector in the States. Linda not only spoke fluent Spanish but knew the local *policía* and the inspectors and was familiar with both the U.S. and the Puerto Rican permitting process. Two hours and forty-five minutes after leaving Tampa, our plane rolled up to the Puerto Rican customs ramp, and Linda was waiting.

When chartering a plane to a foreign country, everyone must remain by the aircraft before passing customs. Normally it doesn't take long, but we lingered outside for hours as commercial airliners rumbled and screeched by, immersing our group in kerosene vapors as we simmered in the noonday sun. Henry, our inspector from the Departmento de Recursos Naturales y Ambientales, was delayed.

I found out later that there were several of his buddies who wanted to see this mountain lion who flew to Puerto Rico in a Lear jet and it took time to get them together. When he and his police friends arrived, they were congenial, courteous, and all smiles, and they wanted pictures of the celebrity cat, who wasn't dusty and windblown like the rest of us. No, he languished on a full-size, leather lounge in a stretch limo with soft music, and iced spring water and munched on Eukanuba cat food.

Finally it was on to our hotel—the Westin Rio Mar Resort Hotel—where Cougar's first-floor room and terrace overlooked meticulously manicured grounds, beaches to die for, and crystal-clear, blue-green Caribbean waters. The hotel décor was half Western, half island, and both the employees and the guests were excited to have Cougar—if for different reasons. The islanders thought Cougar was an American celebrity feline and the vacationers thought he was an exotic island cat. Everywhere he strolled, he drew an audience, so the hotel provided a security team with two-way radios.

But this wasn't a vacation, it was a mission. Unfortunately, the place to meet and greet the upper echelon of the Iams company was not outside, wafted by island breezes. No, the place was a sales convention set up in a large and hot conference room with display booths crammed in. Booths with loudspeakers barked and meowed as the surrounding people circled like reef angelfish. But Cougar knew quiet and cool Bahamian breezes were just outside the room, down the hall, and through the door. So he indulged me for twenty minutes or so, then headed for the beach. I really couldn't blame him.

When Cougar is uncomfortable, I am too. But making me feel better were Clay, Tom, Marty, and Dr. Diane. Clay was compassionate, Tom was family, Marty took control, Diane was charming. And all were gracious and personable, making me feel like family. They understood that a big cat lingering in such feline-unfriendly surroundings was extraordinary, but Cougar never stayed put long enough for me to carry on a conversation. I was beyond disappointed. The next morning, when I joined Jeff and his boss Bruce for breakfast on a hotel terrace, they were smiling.

Bruce is a big man with heart to match. Marketing is his area of expertise, and the way he goes about it—with compassion—is unique. If he were in the military he'd request, not command, his infantrymen to take that hill and they would, not for country but for Bruce. I would later discover that when I disagreed with someone, Bruce, in his quiet manner, would defuse my objections with logical explanations of why whomever I objected to made sense, never why I didn't.

So there we were, three men in paradise, seated on the rim of a breakfast-table-like wheel, deciding how to roll over the competition. Both Bruce and Jeff had briefcases commemorating the sales conference on the table in front of them. When I noticed and commented that they were handsome, Bruce opened the black Naugahyde case with gold lettering, removed his personal effects, and handed it to me. That's Bruce. Next we discussed the upcoming schedule, while Linda remained back at the room, cat-sitting. Yes, Cougar is exciting and opens Lear jet doors and Caribbean shores, but there isn't an instant when I'm not thinking about him. My mind can never be on vacation and forget that a two-hundred-pound cat is back in the room. Linda allows me the luxury and the opportunity to redirect, but never forget, my number one responsibility. Besides, she enjoys spending one-on-one time with her "son."

So after the breakfast meeting and an afternoon of Cougar terrorizing the local birds, it was back into the limo, then the Lear jet, and in three hours we were home. At the St. Petersburg airport I attempted to scoot Cougar into his Suburban. But this time he backed up and looked around. There was no limo. He hesitated. I waited. I nudged. He wouldn't move. Finally, after several minutes of scanning the horizon, he slowly and begrudgingly stepped up and in. Back to reality.

IT WAS SHOW time, and wherever we were, Jeff was, too. Mutual respect was our bond. He knew what Eukanuba needed and I knew what Cougar needed. And the charm of it was, they needed each other. Jeff was innovative and honest. When someone is good, he is promoted. Unfortunately for us, Jeff went to the dogs. (The Iams Company has dog food, too.) I heard that his replacement was allergic to cats.

With Jeff gone, I made a request. I wanted Connie to coordinate the shows. Connie is Bruce's secretary. Connie knows where everything is, what's going on, who everyone is, and how to get things done. She is intelligent, fun to be around, and honorable, and she loves Cougar. What more could I ask?

Normally it was the assistant brand manager like Jeff who oversaw shows, but Bruce, taking my wishes into account, appointed Connie and gave her managerial powers when Cougar was around. I kid her and say that she is older than I because she was born in April and I in June of the same year, but usually she is the one dealing it out. For example, during an outside show in Detroit, Cougar excused himself to take care of "business" in front of the audience. I jokingly held up a towel as a curtain. During the next performance Cougar walked over to the same spot, checked his scent, and grimaced in ecstasy. I explained that he loved his own smell. Connie blurted out, "Like father, like son." The audience collapsed with laughter. Then I responded, "Maybe, but at least I don't taste my urine."

Linda and I were having dinner with Dr. Dan Carey, the director of technical communications, research, and development at Iams, and his wife, Debbie, when I presented him with a question. "From the perspective of Iams Company, what are my top three strengths?" His immediate answer was: sincerity, dedication, and my link with the audience. It made me think. While these attributes have *nothing* to do with Cougar, they reflect the values of the marketplace—those buying Eukanuba cat food and the Iams Company.

We're close, like squadron mates being catapulted off an aircraft carrier for the health and well-being of animals, where culture, customers, products, people . . . and Cougar are important.

10

AS EARTH'S TENANT RULERS,

CAN WE BE PROUD?

BIAS IS OUR worst enemy. Even our religion decrees that we are godlike. We refer to an animal as "it" rather than "he" or "she," and even our Golden Rule refers only to mankind. Why not do unto creatures rather than unto people? It's because the world rotates around power, and wildlife seemingly has little. But it has more than one might think, albeit, seemingly imperceptible.

All things are connected. Yes, we realize that when a tree is cut down something is missing, but it goes much further than that. From air purification to soil erosion to nesting birds, the world has changed.

But who cares? The world will survive, we're told. It's time to take, take as much as we can before someone else does. Acquiring the most defines success. That's why so many people are miserable, because there is always more out there for the insatiable appetite. But actually our glass is now half empty; this planet has little more to give, and by the time we recognize this it may be too late.

My experience with Cougar has taught me this; it has made me realize that I have a responsibility living on this planet. Inner strength helps show the way. When I was a little boy, the

"Just for Today" litany, whose author is unknown, hung on my wall. It listed a dozen or so different rules to work on each and every day. One directive was to do something commendable without being found out. It was a great lesson for achieving inner peace.

When asked if Cougar wouldn't be better off in the "wild," I know I'm addressing someone who hasn't stopped to think. I yearn for a place where Cougar *would* be better off, but there isn't one wildlife area on this planet that isn't riddled with hikers, bikers, motorcycles, four-wheel vehicles, and ATVs. To all the surrounding animals, these noisy, smelly, two-legged creatures are trespassing. Modern-day pseudoconquistadors believe they're in the wild, but they're not, not anymore. Hordes of humans recreate while talking on cell phones, enveloping wildlife in exhaust fumes, and depositing cigarette butts, jagged cans, food wrappers, and broken bottles. To these trash-throwing trespassers the outdoors appears litter free, but they're using how things are back home as example.

The wilderness may seem boundless, but when you must endure life there, call it home, the vastness quickly disappears. It takes a lot of land for a predator at the top of the food chain to survive. Take man. How much property does it take to feed, clothe, house, medicate, and entertain him? Take another predator, the big cat. Depending on prey density and cover, one male mountain lion requires between twenty-five and five hundred square miles for basic survival. That's for *one* male lion. Characteristically, there are several females residing within his territory, so for the sake of simplicity, let's say a hundred square miles are required for every cat.

Let's optimistically assume for a moment that every mountain lion has a hundred square miles of littered land to call home. Now spin a web of roads, erect electrical towers, throw up wooden and chain-link fences, and lay miles upon miles of slashing barbed wire. And our menacing is not yet over. Each leaf and every blade of grass are dusted with filth, the air stinks, the water is cloudy and tastes pungent. To us the air smells fresh and clean, but that's compared to driving on the freeway using a nose that doesn't work.

As if this weren't enough, out of nowhere, coming from everywhere, humans encroach further, some with guns and most with junk food. Many people think that by feeding a bear they are helping the bear, but they might as well shoot him. The bear becomes used to handouts and approaches other vacationers for the same treatment. Eventually, someone will feel threatened and complain that this bear is too forward, is not apprehensive of people, so in the name of humanity it's time to shoot a new friend of man, calling him too dependent for his own good. It's all right for bears to be out in the open so that vacationers can see them, but it's unacceptable for them to get too close—an artificial line drawn by man.

These leafy locations are balanced ecosystems, not just places for us to go to get away from it all. If Cougar had lived in such a place, he would have been lucky to make it to his fourth birthday without being either shot by a hunter or hit by a car. Four years in the "wild" is probably better for the cat than being crammed in a cage . . . until the age of four. But there is an alternative: we can really make it better by—at the risk of sounding trite—being compassionate.

That's easier said than done. We *are* compassionate, aren't we? Don't dare call us anything else! Smokers don't give it a second thought and consider themselves compassionate when they flick a cigarette butt onto the ground. Don't tell them otherwise. There's no law against it—at least none that is enforced. But there are billions of people doing the same thing. Our world is finite and getting smaller. It wasn't long ago that pioneers moved farther into the wilderness because they could see their neighbors' chimney smoke. If only they knew.

So what is compassion? I'm using the word *compassion* to mean more than empathy or sympathy, to express a shared interest in the plight of our planet and all life on it, a dedication to help—one step beyond saying, "Gosh, that's too bad" to concern that says, "And I'm going to help." But again this is easier said than done.

Predators don't like predators. Man is the worst example, exterminating wildlife predators, calling it "sport" or "harvesting," or saying it is "necessary." In less than a century man single-handedly has all but wiped out most of the top predators, not with his brawn, but with what he calls brains. Unfortunately, the right hand doesn't know what the left one is doing. For instance, the Florida panther has endangered status and is protected by human law while Texas cougars are considered vermin and shot. Will we ever learn? Do we have to virtually annihilate something before deciding to rescue it? Is this our way?

The mountain lion has been one of the fortunate few, surviving man's selfishness better than most. But people aren't selfish, are they? So we stay on this course until man eventually recognizes the error of his ways. Someday soon we may purchase aerosol cans of mountain air, as we now buy bottles of water. Don't laugh. It wasn't long ago when everyone would have mocked the idea of buying spring water.

THE FIRST STEPS in making a change are the most difficult. We must realize that hunting and teaching our sons and daughters to hunt is not sport but misplaced aggression—inappropriate, unfair, and destructive of the biosphere. Why not spend the time taking pictures? It takes a lot more talent. How much genius, strength, and courage does it require to remain quiet, point a high-powered rifle, and pull the trigger? And who gets all warm inside admiring a decapitated head on the wall? We must acknowledge that just because we are able to slay a mountain lion, wolf, or bear doesn't mean we are better than the animal; it just means that the gun gave us a misused and misguided advantage. The gun has no brains; turn it around and the same plight would befall the hunter. Guns make weak people strong. They're a crutch, and the slaughter continues for two reasons—the need to feel superior and the ability to get away with it—both human frailties. And let's not rationalize that killing wildlife for food makes it okay. It all boils down to the thrill of killing, and eating the victims just adds insult to the injury.

Philosophically, sharing this planet with wildlife predators could be like driving to work. Not paying attention when you're driving is dangerous; being aware makes it safe. The same principle applies to sharing this planet with wildlife. Unfortunately, many people are mentally lazy; they don't want to think. And why should they? They aren't the ones who suffer. This planet is no one's or everyone's; either way, hunting is stealing. When we destroy a car, two will take its place, but when wildlife is lost, it takes a generation to replace—if it can be replaced at all. We are selectively destroying irreplaceable pieces of an intricate puzzle and rationalizing all the way. Flick a cigarette, build a shopping center, construct a road, drain a swamp, build a house, shoot a bear. What's the big deal? The big deal is that most of the entire burgeoning human population is doing it.

I'm a realist; man will continue to encroach; it's his nature. But my hope is that in so doing, he will learn to be a good neighbor with wildlife, if not for the animals' sake, then for his own.

There are a number of ways to do so. When it comes to wildlife cats, there are two main rules: Stand and Stare. It's even easier than learning to drive.

Cats, big and small, are curious. When you bring something new home or change the location of a trinket, your cat is the first to notice. It's his curiosity.

So one day you might be strolling through the woods and spy a mountain lion, cougar, catamount, puma, or panther (as you know, they're all the same cat). There is a mixture of awe and hesitation, maybe even fright. But in the last century, there have only been twelve fatal attacks by American lions. That's a little more than one fatality a decade. We are thousands of times more likely to get struck by lightning, yet still we walk in the rain. So why not walk with wildlife? As a matter of fact, worldwide, herbivores claim more human lives than carnivores.

Subtract all the sensationalism and we just have a curious cat. Someone, namely you, is pussyfooting through his territory and he's inquisitive. Are you friend or foe? It's only second nature for him to be cautious. In the same situation you would be, too.

Besides, you are standing vertically, and that makes you appear bigger than you really are; you are intimidating. He doesn't want confrontation, so he crouches to stay out of sight but continues sniffing, scanning, and listening. When people view a big cat crouching, they get nervous, but attack is the last thing on his mind. He just wants to be inconspicuous.

At first both you and the cat are still. The correct thing for you to do is slowly and quietly back up and walk away. But many humans have brain-fade, so they turn and run. In this case, the cat no longer sees you as a threat. You are, after all, running away, and, from his point of view, very slowly. Hunger would heighten his excitement but has little to do with this curiosity, for you don't fit the image of prey; you're just strange, standing or moving on two legs rather than four. This scenario happens thousands of times a year with no other result than someone spinning a wildlife tale. But why take the chance?

It's a fact that cats hate confrontation. If you and the cat are in a standoff, rather than turning yourself into a toy, act tough. Raise your arms; speak the cat's language and hiss. And if the cat doesn't move, throw something, wildly waving your arms and hissing loudly; even charge forward several steps. It's the same hoax hunting dogs use. They bark and rush. There is only one time this will not work and that is if the cat is a mother with kittens nearby. In this rare situation you want out of there just as much as she does. So oblige her by backing up without turning around, then at twenty or thirty yards, turn around and— periodically looking over your shoulder—slowly walk away.

You have indisputable powers: standing and staring. No cat will test you. And remember, motion rapidly traveling away is stim-

AS EARTH'S TENANT RULERS, CAN WE BE PROUD?   225

ulating for him and a sudden motion toward him is intimidating. Also, height is an advantage; being above a cat is much better than being below him. Mountain lions aren't known to spring from a perch like leopards, but Cougar does get a kick out of just jumping from the second-story deck. He never has leapt *onto* something; he just leaps for the fun of it.

Follow these rules and you won't be attacked, but all this knowledge depends on knowing that a big cat is there. Most of the time a big cat will see you and you won't see the cat, and nothing happens. But in that billion-to-one case where you are attacked by a mountain lion: *Face the cat, don't turn around, protect the back of your neck, and fight back with everything you've got.* Rolling up into a little ball may work with bears, but not with cats. It's time to poke him in the nose and scratch his eyes.

Stop for a moment and think about house cats. How do you call them closer? Get on their level, maybe talk in high-pitched tones. And what scares them? A rapid motion toward them is always threatening. Big cats are no different. The things that attract and that scare Kitty will have the same effect on wildlife lions. So when confronted by a big cat out in the "wild," stand tall, wave your arms, shout, hiss. Try to think of him as a big kitty cat, because he is.

Many states recommend picking up a child when a mountain lion is near, but that recommendation applies only with babies. With toddlers, it's best to gather them close to you. The lion can easily differentiate between an adult and a child, so nothing is accomplished by picking up a child other than that the adult is thrown off balance, is strained, and moves less fluidly. Cats are body-language experts. Therefore the best course is to stand next to children, keep them quiet, and act intimidating.

One more tip: Cats are scent-driven, and there is a fragrance that Cougar adores—insect repellent. He'll purr, smearing my leg with little saliva bubbles. That could be a little disconcerting if a wildlife lion did the same to you.

IN CLOSING, I want to share a relevant question I am frequently asked when Cougar is present: Is he tame? The answer is at the core of this book. "Tame" is in the eye of the beholder. Are small children tame when they carry guns to school? Are you tame when someone threatens your family? When it comes to jealousy, guarding, protecting, or just being scared, the lion is no different. What is unfair is that lions are called wild when they act identically to humans. When people act the same way, we just attach a long scientific name to it, saying it's understandable; for lions it's "wild." The truth of the matter is that man is no better at controlling himself than a beast is. Lashing out is a way of life. Man certainly is not tame. Television, newspapers, and magazines are soaked in blood—pictures and print portraying man's inhumanity to man and animal alike. And we call lions wild.

Getting along with people and with lions relies on the same principles: Press the good behavioral buttons and don't act stupid. And there is no way on God's still-green earth that sensationalism, myth, illusion, and fantasy can guide us into making the correct decisions. We even rationalize killing. We must objectively question what wild really means. Are lions wild or is labeling them so like shrugging our shoulders and admitting that we don't know? It wasn't long ago that lion tamers were armed with whips. So we're gaining on it.

Increasingly, we attempt to understand why another person acts violently. Is it caused by drugs, an abusive childhood, extreme frustration, or just not caring? All of these feelings can be overwhelming. But at least we are concerned, we empathize, and we try to comprehend human behavior. This is better than our approach to animals: We label animals as "some*thing*" wild and, while acting hypocritically pompous, just turn our backs on them. We need instead to be concerned. We need to be compassionate. Animals are not "things." Just look through their eyes.

IT WAS EARLY morning, four days before Valentine's Day
2001, when Linda and I discovered that Cougar was having difficulty breathing. We quickly drove our feline sweetheart to the
University of Gainesville Veterinary Hospital for tests. And at
the conclusion of a rather long diagnostic process, which for
large cats includes general anesthesia, they flipped Cougar over
and suddenly his heart went into cardiac fibrillation. Then, just
as suddenly, it returned to a normal rhythm and he was carted
off to recovery. His medical team and anesthesiologist removed
monitoring machines and oxygen as Linda and I just tried to
stay out of the way. Finally, Cougar was disconnected from his
intubation tube (the tube keeping his windpipe free and clear)
and on his own. Everyone was cleaning up and trying, at last,
to relax. His anesthesiologist, relieved that the crisis was over,
glanced down again and noticed that Cougar wasn't breathing.
She quickly confirmed the worst: He had no pulse.

The intubation tube was rammed back down his windpipe,
quickly connected to the anesthesia machine, and a technician
began squeezing and releasing the anbu bag as his doctor, with
the heel of his hand, repeatedly compressed Cougar's chest every
second. Technicians delivered a constant stream of loaded syrin-
ges and swabs, which were administered and flung back as empty
plastic cylinders and wads of blood-soiled gauze. After ten

minutes with no pulse, Cougar's doctor gave up, got up, and walked over to Linda and me, saying, "This is not good. The only thing left now is to saw down his sternum, crack open his ribs, and manipulate his heart, but I wouldn't advise it." I blared back, "Whatever it takes, but you're wasting valuable time explaining all this. Get back with Cougar."

Somewhere between injecting epinephrine directly into Cougar's heart and administering dopamine-saline solution into his femoral artery, Cougar showed positive signs. His pulse, at first feeble, grew in intensity until he was back. Three board-certified doctors and three technicians were out of breath saving this little guy—who is more important to me than life itself. A hush fell over them. No one had ever experienced anything like this. I could hear the whispers: This was a miracle.

It is policy that Cougar remain at the hospital. Would Cougar really benefit from being confined in a cage, abandoned and scared, even with someone knowledgeable checking in on him every hour or so? Or would he be better off at home, comfortable, constantly monitored by me? Most people would choose the hospital, but I'm not most people. After signing waivers and brushing up on our cat CPR, it was late when Linda drove home with Cougar in the back with me. He was wobbly, he was sore, he was disorientated. He rocked, swayed, and circled, then plopped down into my lap and fell asleep. I stroked his glistening coat, now checkered with shaved patches of bare skin, and began reflecting.

All animals tenaciously hold on to life, by instinct; it is only humans who realize the finality of it all. And somehow even our knowledge that death is an absolute doesn't make it any easier.

The only consolation may be in knowing we've given love and were loved in return, that we've had a positive reason for being, that we've made a difference. As mountain lions go, Cougar has accomplished all this and more. I'm so proud of him.

We frequently don't appreciate the important things. We get caught up in the miniscule, mundane nature of everyday life and don't savor the very essence of what makes us happy. I don't think I will ever again be irritated when Cougar "misses" his box or gets me up at three in the morning. I will *savor* every second we are together, realizing it could be our last. Yes, Cougar lives. He still has more to teach me. And I'm a slow learner.